THE
S CHOOL-LEAVER'S
HANDBOOK

THE SCHOOL-LEAVER'S HANDBOOK

The Indispensable Guide to Life After 16

Edited by
Stephen Adamson
and
Jacquie Hughes

Foreword by
Sankha Guha

BLOOMSBURY

First published by Adamson Books 1986
This revised edition published 1990

Copyright © Adamson Books 1990
Bloomsbury Publishing Limited
2 Soho Square, London W1V 5DE

Cover design by Lawrence Bradbury
Book design by Judith Robertson
Cartoons by Jerry Glover
ISBN 0 7475 0681 7

British Library Cataloguing in Publication Data
A CIP record for this book is available
from the British Library

10 9 8 7 6 5 4 3 2 1

Typeset by Goodfellow & Egan of Cambridge

CONTENTS

ACKNOWLEDGEMENTS

The first edition of *The School-leaver's Handbook* was compiled and edited by Jacquie Hughes, whose enthusiasm, commitment and hard work inspired everyone who worked on the project and laid the ground-work for all future editions. In addition, thanks are due to the individual contributors for their time, expertise and interest: Anne Ashworth (Money Matters); Christine Ball (Self-Employment and Unemployment); Colin Byrne (Continuing Your Education); Helen Dady (Politics); Alison Holbourn (Looking After Yourself); Jacquie Hughes (Living At Home and Using Your Time); Melanie McFadyean (Relationships); Heather Macrae (Employment); Sarah Marten (Continuing Your Education); Steve Pinder (Politics); Anthony Rose (The Law); Owen Watson (Getting Around); Christian Wolmar (Moving Away).

We would also like to thank Sankha Guha for his enthusiastic and thoughtful Foreword and Jerry Glover for lightening the load with his cartoons. Thanks are also due to Judith Robertson and Lawrence Bradbury for their designs, Judith Iles for her advice, Daisy Hayden for constant interest and ideas and Kathy Rooney for supporting this new edition.

FOREWORD

This is a very important book. You may have noticed that it is sub-titled 'The Indispensable Guide to Life after 16' – and that means most of your life. Furthermore, forget the sentimental myths; it is life after school that should give you 'the best years of your life'. There will be plenty of time one day for you to look back at your early teens through rosy tints, to forget about the frustrations and petty rules which cramped your style.

For the moment, as a school-leaver you aren't interested in looking back; the future holds all the possibilities you've only half dreamt of. The most tantalizing word in your vocabulary now is 'independence'. Independence from school, teachers, parents and home. You would be less than human if the changes you're facing didn't worry you just a little. Your world has become larger and infinitely more complex.

It's easy to get intimidated. What do you know about signing on? At what age can you be imprisoned or become a market trader? At what age can you drive a heavy goods vehicle or consent to a homosexual act? What is APR? What is a 'grievance procedure' on the YTS? What are your rights as a tenant?

The answers are all here, and if that frightens you even more, the good news is that this isn't a text book. You don't have to learn it by rote and you won't be tested on it. As in all good reference books the information here is easy to locate when the need for it arises (you won't have to become an expert on the Common Market if what you are interested in is yoga). The reading list and database of contacts and organizations at the back mean that further inquiry on a given subject is painless. Above all there is no waffle or condescension, but a down-to-earth emphasis on hard facts.

A final point. Since the first edition of this handbook there have been many changes. One of the opening lines in the 1986 edition was 'You might be worried that you are never going to get a job at all.' As the nineties progress the effects of what has come to be known as the 'Demographic Timebomb' will be felt increasingly, and that line will hopefully become obsolete. Basically, as a dip in the birth-rate of 1970s feeds through into the 1990s, school-leavers will become scarcer. You will become prized commodities. So let me return to my theme – this is an important book, not simply because of what it contains. Ultimately it's an important book because you are important. Use it.

SANKHA GUHA
Manchester, 1990

E|MPLOYMENT

For many school-leavers the prospect of saying good-bye to the classroom and going to a job is an exciting one. No more sitting at desks learning, but instead responsibility, equality, new people to meet and things to do, and above all the enticing prospect of the pay packet or cheque at the end of the week or month. Even though this new life will also have its fair share of the humdrum and its times of frustration, it is certainly going to be different from what you are used to, and there will be a lot of initial adjustments to make.

Those leaving school without a clear idea of what they are going to do, or maybe thinking that they will be unemployed, might feel tempted to flip over these pages. Well don't rush by! There are various things you can do to maximise your chance of employment – and you are almost certainly more skilled and eligible than you imagine. Read on . . .

Choosing a career

You've probably already given a lot of thought to this, and discussed it with your careers teachers at school. If not, and you're still at school, it's not too late. See them and get as much information out of them as you can, and talk to lots of other people about their jobs and what qualifications you might need if a job takes your fancy. If you've left school, or are on the point of leaving, go to your local Careers Office, and also try out the other sources of job ideas (see pp. 48–50). If you're at college talk to the college careers officer.

Being positive can make a lot of difference to your self-esteem as well as your job prospects. Whatever criticisms you may have been subjected to by others, or even by yourself, you still have

9

excellent skills and abilities which could get you the job you want. Write them down, think about them and be prepared to use them when discussing employment. Too much modesty will get you nowhere.

Getting the job

Once you have found jobs to apply for, you face the task of getting one. There are a lot of myths surrounding the 'curriculum vitae' you might be asked for, application forms you'll have to fill in and the interview you'll have to attend. Don't panic. First imagine yourself in the position of an employer and think about what *you* would like to know about a prospective employee and how you would find out. You might find that it all seems clearer.

The 'curriculum vitae' (CV) or 'personal profile'

Once you have answered an advertisement for a job you might also be asked for your 'curriculum vitae' or CV, or you may have to send one with your application. 'Curriculum vitae' literally means your life history, and is a common means of gaining information about a job applicant. This is the first way that

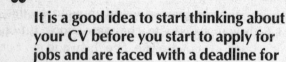

66

It is a good idea to start thinking about your CV before you start to apply for jobs and are faced with a deadline for your application.

99

employers will find out about you, so you need to give a strong image of yourself and make them interested in you. Be glad of the chance to write a CV. It can allow you more freedom to give personal details in an original way.

It is a good idea to start thinking about your CV before you start to apply for jobs and are faced with a deadline for your application. You can use it to help you fill in forms, and once you have done it, you won't have to scratch your head each time to remember the dates you attended various schools, the holiday jobs you've done and exams you might have taken. A well organised CV is much better than a long, rambling letter recounting your life story. Always keep a few copies, preferably on good photocopying paper. You never know when you might need it.

The following headings will be useful in helping you organise facts about yourself:

- Name, full address, telephone number.
- Date of birth, age.
- Schools attended: Name, address, dates.
- Colleges attended: Name, address, dates.
- Qualifications (if any): Name of examinations, subjects, grades. Other certificates, e.g. music.
- Previous employment: Include Saturday and holiday jobs, part-time work, dates.
- Voluntary work: Include any community activities, campaigns, fund-raising.
- Interests: Put them all down. Watching television counts, particularly if you can talk about certain sorts of programmes you enjoy.
- Future training or education plans: Mention evening classes or courses you are taking, and any other subjects you would like to follow. Are they leading to something else you want to do?
- Referees: Give the names of two people in responsible positions who know you, such as teachers, past employers, youth workers, church ministers, or just neighbours. It's polite to ask them first, and also wise as they might be written to by potential employers to ask them their assessment of you.

Give as much relevant detail as possible, but do not include anything you won't be able to talk about at an interview. Type your CV if you can. If not, write it clearly.

Application forms

You may find that you are sent an application form which asks for the same information as a CV even though you have already sent a CV in which you put your soul on paper. The points to remember are the same as above. You may be asked, 'Why have you applied for this post?' and other specific questions which aim to discover how you would tackle the job.

Do not simply write the answers you think the employer will want to hear. Everyone else will be doing that too. Try to make points in an original way, without straying from what you actually feel. Whatever you do, avoid one-word answers. If necessary, add a sheet of paper to the form. But try not to ramble, as you won't want the reader to fall asleep either.

Recently some 'equal opportunities' employers have included a question about the racial background of applicants. This is part of the 'ethnic monitoring' process which, it is argued, is necessary to find out the position of black and national minority people in the workforce and to monitor their progress from the date of applying. You will usually have the choice whether to answer this question.

Going for the interview

Hopefully, your carefully-written CV and application form will have done the trick, and you'll be invited for an interview. Try and see this as an opportunity to find out more about the job and the workplace, as well as to talk about yourself. This '11 Point Plan' should help you.

1 As soon as you get the interview invitation, note down the time, who you are going to see, and work out how to get there. Don't forget to confirm that you will be attending.

2 Find out as much as you can about the firm beforehand. Ask a careers teacher or advisor, go to the local reference library and talk to people you know who work there.

3 Dealing with nerves on the day is never easy, but most

people find that being a bit nervous helps to sharpen up their responses. Don't worry if you are a bit on edge, as the interviewer will expect it. Try to get a good night's sleep beforehand to help you relax.

4 Practice interviews can help a lot, particularly with someone who does similar work. You will be prepared for most of the questions asked. The following are usual: 'Tell me a bit about yourself; why do you want this job?'; 'Why do you think you would be good at it?'; 'How do you spend your spare time?'; 'What is your ambition?'; 'Where would you like to end up in this company?'

5 Be prepared for a test. It might be a simple English and arithmetic test, or one to try your manual skills. If you have not thought about it, you might be thrown into a panic. If you get stuck, move on and come back to the difficult part. You won't be expected to be perfect.

6 Don't be late. Employers will not be impressed if they think you will never turn up for work on time, so leave some extra time to allow for the deficiencies of public transport. Being late won't get you off to a calm start either.

7 Wear clothes you feel comfortable in. That new backless sundress might just make you feel self-conscious. Play down the outrageous.

8 Once in the room, sit down – when you're asked. Remember the interviewer's name and use it. It can help to break down the feeling of distance and unequal power between you, but don't use his or her first name unless the interviewer asks you to, and don't smoke unless invited to.

Remember that the interviewer wants to find out about you. Tell yourself this before you start answering. Don't mumble, and look at who you are talking to.

9 Watch the reactions of the person you're talking to. If you're talking too much, or not to the point, it will show. Expand on things which catch his or her interest.

10 Ask questions where appropriate. You have an equal right to know about your prospective workplace.

11 If you are offered the job on the spot, don't be afraid to ask for time to think it over. Ask about pay, hours, holidays, overtime, training and promotion opportunities. If you have a disability talk about facilities you will need.

Discrimination and prejudice

The Race Relations Act and the Sex Discrimination Act make it illegal for an employer, trade union or employment agency to discriminate against you because of your race, sex or colour. This applies to recruitment as well as the conditions of work.

If you don't get an interview it is very difficult to prove that you were discriminated against on these grounds, though you would have a good case, say, if you are a woman and you discovered that several women had applied for the job but none had been offered an interview. But a possible employer does not have to tell you that you have been rejected because you are black or a woman to be breaking the law. However, if you're black, and a white person with the same qualifications as you is given the job, the employer might be acting illegally.

If you do go to an interview and there is obvious hostility to you because of your race or sex, you would have a good case for claiming discrimination. If you think that you have suffered racial or sexual discrimination, go to a local law centre, women's centre, a Citizens Advice Bureau (CAB) or the local Community Relations Council (find them in the telephone book). They will approach the employer, and if they get no satisfactory response, with their support you could take your case to a tribunal which will decide whether your claim is justified. You must do this within three months of the incident.

It is also discrimination if a condition for employment is made which prevents certain groups from qualifying, such as arbitrary restrictions on head-dress at work which would automatically prevent Sikhs from obtaining the job. On the other hand, there have to be certain exceptions for gender, such as a part in a play that required a male actor, or jobs requiring a particular sex for reasons of privacy or decency.

Starting work

Moving from unemployment, college or school work is not always the glorious transition it sounds, but it can be exciting. At school the older people were in positions of authority over you, but in a job you will find people of all different ages who are regarded as equals. Particularly when you start you would be unlucky if you did not find that most of your colleagues, whether older than you or not, are welcoming and friendly. You may also find that your superior is quite happy to be friendly and maybe have a drink with you after hours, though it is advisable to be cautious at first about how familiar to be with your bosses at work. Of course, there will be someone who patronises you as the 'new boy/girl' or who takes on the role of office bully, but it won't last long and you probably won't remember the first day's nerves by the end of the week.

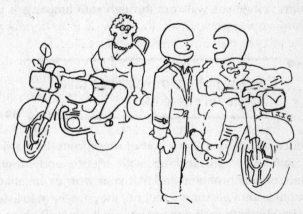

"That's Mrs Wilson. I work with her in accounts."

You will have less constant direction than you (hopefully) had at school, and will be expected to get down to the job. Being paid for what you're doing makes a lot of difference to the way you're treated. However, don't be frightened to ask questions. It's far better to be clear about the job from the start and no-one will expect you to be perfect. Mistakes will be expected, so it's better to confess them than to try to cover them up. It is a good idea not to be late if you can possibly avoid it. It will do nothing for your self-esteem or prospects to be branded as unreliable from the start.

One of the first things you will notice is the different rhythm of a day's work from a day at school. For one thing, the day is longer, most working days being about eight hours. Lunch will only be an hour, or even a little less, and you may get a tea break each morning and afternoon, but if you work at a desk you may have to take tea or coffee while you work.

From school you will be used to having your day broken into periods during which you did specific tasks, but at work you may spend all day doing the same job, or find that you are being switched from task to task. Either way, the new pattern of work can take some getting used to, and you can expect to feel tired after a day's work. At least there is the compensation of no homework; when you walk out through your employer's doors, your time's your own.

66
The new pattern of work can take some getting used to.
99

If it does not all look like a bed of roses from the start, don't panic. Talk over your feelings with friends and other new workers. You will probably find that your worries are shared. If the company has a personnel section, they are there to listen, so talk to somebody there if none of your colleagues is able to help you sort them out.

Your wage packet

As most companies pay for work done, rather than in advance, you will probably wait a week, or even a month, before your first payment. You may have to wait a further week or month if your company pays 'in hand', which means they hold your first pay packet until you leave. This is intended to stop people just walking out of a job. When it does come you will receive the famous pay slip, which is actually an itemised pay statement.

If you are a manual worker you are entitled to payment in cash, in which case the slip will arrive in an envelope with your money, but if you work in an office you will probably be paid by cheque or have payment made directly into your bank or building society account (see pp. 89–96), and just receive the slip. The slip shows your gross wages – the amount you earn before tax – and your net wages – what you get once deductions have been made – together with all the deductions, and methods and amounts of payment if you are not paid all your wages in the same way. You are not entitled to a wage slip if you work less than eight hours a week, and if you work between eight and 16 hours you only get them after five years' continuous employment, although in both cases some employers do supply wage slips.

Your main deductions will be income tax and National Insurance. As a wage-earner, these are regarded as your contributions towards running the country, including services such as the National Health Service and education. National Insurance will guarantee you basic income in the case of unemployment, sickness, maternity or industrial injury. It also counts towards your State retirement pension.

Income tax

As an employee you will be on the Pay As You Earn (PAYE) scheme, which means that your employer deducts the tax from your wages before he pays you. For an explanation of income tax and how it is calculated, see pp. 98–9.

National Insurance

National Insurance (NI) will be the other automatic deduction from your wages. Everyone who earns more than a small amount in the financial year, which begins on 6 April, pays contributions. These 'Lower Earnings Limits' were £43 weekly and £187 monthly for the year ending 5 April 1990; your employer or local Department of Social Security (DSS) office will tell you the current limits. If you earn more than these figures you will pay 2 per cent on the first £43 per week you earn and then 9 per cent thereafter, unless your company is 'contracted out' of the State pension scheme (see SERPS opposite), in which case the rate is 7 per cent. Your employer makes an additional contribution for you. The NI year is the same as the tax year.

Benefits you will receive when unemployed, sick, injured, pregnant, or retired will depend on the number of NI contributions you have credited to you and the type of contribution you have paid. There are four classes of these, Class 1 being those usually paid by ordinary employees. To get full benefits at present you must have paid NI on 50 times the Lower Earnings Limit in the relevant tax year. The 'relevant tax year' is the last complete one, i.e. for 1990, it was 6 April 1988 to 5 April 1989. For 1991, it will be 6 April 1989 to 5 April 1990. However, if you have only paid 25 times the Lower Earnings Limit, you may still be entitled to some benefits. As a 'new' worker, you will not be entitled to receive benefits based on NI contributions immediately. If you are registered unemployed or sick, receiving industrial injury or invalidity benefit, on a full-time government sponsored training course, or in full-time education and are over 18, you will get full Class 1 contributions credited to you even though you haven't paid them.

Everyone between the ages of 16 and 60 (women) and 65 (men) is allocated a National Insurance number which they have to quote when claiming benefits. Since 1975 every new applicant for a number has had to produce their passport or birth certificate as proof of identity.

If you have any queries about your NI contributions you should ring your local office, which is listed under 'Health and Social Security – Pensions, National Insurance and General Enquiries' in the telephone directory.

Pensions and superannuation

You may think it a little premature to start thinking about retirement, but once you start to pay National Insurance you are already contributing to your old age through the State retirement pension scheme.

There are two kinds of pension: the State ones and private or 'contracted out' schemes operating in your workplace. Pensions are often extremely complicated and it is worth investigating them early if you think you will want a better pension than the State offers you when you retire.

State pensions

At present there are two State pensions: the basic pension, and an additional, earnings-related one. The basic pension is based on payment of National Insurance contributions. To get a full State pension, about nine tenths of your working life must count as 'reckonable years' for National Insurance purposes, that is years in which you paid contributions on 50 times the Lower Earnings Limit mentioned earlier. The actual pension, when you receive it, is small (the full rates at the time of writing are £43.60 for a single person for those with full contributions, or £69.80 for a married pensioner).

In addition, since 1978 there has been a State Additional Earnings Related Pension (SERPS) scheme, which was modified in the mid-1980s. The idea behind it was to provide a good addition to the basic pension. All workers earning more than the Lower Earnings Limit have to contribute, along with their employers, either to SERPS or to private Additional Earnings Related Pensions Schemes. Calculation of SERPS is complicated, but it is now basically intended to guarantee those who will retire after 2010 an additional pension equivalent to a fifth of their average annual salary, adjusted to allow for inflation.

Private pensions

Many firms operate private pension schemes; often they have

been negotiated by trade unions. These schemes have to meet various standards. Companies that have such schemes are deemed to have 'contracted out' of the State scheme, and if you are in one your National Insurance will be reduced to offset your 'superannuation', or private pension payments. However, you are not restricted by whether your employer has a separate scheme: you can 'contract out' of SERPS and joint a private scheme of your choice. If you do this you still have the option of 'contracting in' again into SERPS. In reality, a private pension is just deferred pay, usually with additional benefits which vary according to the scheme. Whereas you contribute to SERPS from the age of 16, you do not join most private schemes until you are 21.

Your rights at work

Even if you are delighted to have got work, remember that no-one is doing you a favour by 'giving' you a job – you are going to be providing work for your employer, and are entitled to various rights in return. The laws governing these are complicated, and the following is only an outline of the main ones.

Duties on you and your employer

The provisions of various laws of the country contribute to your contract of employment and impose general duties upon you and your employer: his or her duties include paying you and providing safe working conditions. In turn, you must work, co-operate, obey reasonable instructions within your contract and be trustworthy. This means that you must do the work you have been employed to do and behave responsibly. In addition, there will be more explicit conditions spelled out in the terms of your employment.

Contract of employment

As soon as you accept the offer of a job, you will have entered into a 'contract' with your employer. A contract of employment is a legal agreement – written or verbal (it can even consist of both a verbal and written agreement) – between you and your employer. Although you may have a single contract covering everything, it is quite likely that the terms of your employment are contained in a variety of documents, notably your letter of appointment, the collective agreement between your employer and union, your job description, written contract, written statement of the main terms and conditions, a verbal agreement, work rules and wage council awards, and established custom and practice in your trade.

Written statement of conditions

All workers working more than 16 hours weekly have the right, within 13 weeks of starting, to a written statement of the main terms and conditions of their job. If you work at least eight hours but less than 16 hours per week you are entitled to it after five years. The statement must include:

- Your name and employer's name
- Title of job, and place of work
- Date employment began
- Expiry of contract if for a fixed term
- Rate of pay and timing of payments
- Hours of work
- Holidays and holiday pay
- Sick pay – if any
- Pension schemes – if any
- Length of notice
- Trade union rights
- Grievance procedure
- Disciplinary procedures.

The written statement is not a contract, and you do not have to sign it. But if you do (as your employer may insist), this will be seen to be strong evidence that you intended it to be considered as a complete statement of the terms of your contract of employment. It cannot be changed without your agreement.

If you do not receive the statement when you should, you can take your employer to an industrial tribunal to ask it to determine what statement you should have been given.

If you feel your employer has broken your contract by, for instance, dismissing you without the correct notice or pay or holiday pay, you can take it up with the employer, or with your trade union. If you do not get satisfaction you can sue in the County Court to recover what you should have been paid. (Further information on industrial tribunals and courts is given in 'The Law' chapter.)

Low pay and the wages councils

Those over 21 have various legal rights with regard to wages, apart from the itemised pay statement. One of these rights is to fixed minimum pay levels and conditions of work in certain low-paying industries – hairdressing, catering, retail shops and stores (but not chemists and butchers), clothing manufacture, laundries, and toy manufacturers. Wages Council agreements determine special minimum rates in these areas. However, since 1986 these protections have been removed from young people.

Equal pay and work of equal value

On average, men earn more than women. Under the Equal Pay Act, 1970, and the 1983 Amendment Regulation to it, women can claim equal pay with men, including overtime rates, sick pay schemes and benefits. You have this right from the first day of working, and regardless of the number of women employed.

To claim equal pay, you have to prove to an industrial tribunal that you are paid less for work which is broadly similar to that being done by a man, or that your work has been given the same rating in a job evaluation scheme. You will need help in preparing your case from your union, a law centre or women's centre. The National Council for Civil Liberties (NCCL) and Equal Opportunities Commission will take test cases and have a lot of experience so it is also worth talking to them.

The new regulations are designed to cover the situation where men are paid better than women doing different jobs, but where the women's work is worth as much as the men's. You can now claim equal pay in this situation. For instance, a woman cook who compared herself with better-paid sheet metal workers won her case. You could also be successful if your job was not

Under the Equal Pay Act, women can claim equal pay with men, including overtime rates, sick pay schemes and benefits.

rated as having equal value under a job evaluation scheme, but you prove that the scheme was discriminatory, or if an independent assessor and a tribunal consider your work of equal value.

Racial discrimination

It is also against the law to be discriminated against on the grounds of race or colour. If, for example, you are black and find that white people no better qualified than you are being preferred for promotion you should take up the matter with your union, if you are a member of one, or with a law centre or local Community Relations Council. Your employer could be liable to prosecution under the Race Relations Act.

Hours of work

In general, your hours of work are laid down in your contract. Until recently in certain jobs the hours you may work before the age of 18 were restricted by various laws, including the Factories Act and the Shops Act.

This protection was removed by the Employment Act 1989, which did away with all special protection on hours given to young people, partially in response to European Commission complaints that the previous laws discriminated between the sexes.

The only exception is shop work, and here the same laws

apply to all workers, namely that you cannot be made to work for more than 6 hours without a 20 minute break, and you must be given three quarters of an hour or more for lunch if you work between 10.30 am and 2.30 pm.

However, wherever you work your employer has to provide a safe working environment. If your hours are too long, then tiredness may make your work unsafe. Contact your union or get legal advice if you think that the hours you are working are making you tired and jeopardising your safety.

Holidays

Your holidays should be laid down in your statement of conditions. In general, workers have no legal right to paid or unpaid holiday, not even on Bank Holidays, though all companies give holidays and trade unions have always negotiated improvements.

Health and safety at work

There are several laws which lay down your rights to work in healthy and safe conditions. Put together they make a complicated package and you will need advice on which apply to you.

The Health and Safety at Work Act, 1974, says that your employer should ensure the 'health, safety and welfare' of all employees by seeing that machinery or equipment at the workplace are safe and that you receive information and training to do your work safely. There should also be a first aid kit, cloakroom space and an accident book in which all accidents are noted down. You can call in a Health and Safety Inspector at any time if you are unhappy with safety conditions.

In addition, you may have an official health and safety representative (HSR) in your workplace, but only where there is a trade union recognised by your employer. An HSR has the right to investigate health hazards, carry out inspections and represent other workers with your employer on health and safety matters. He or she has the right to time off to carry out these duties and for training, as well as facilities for doing the job.

Trade unions

A trade union is an organisation of workers, independent of employers, which exists to protect and promote the rights of its members. Most independent unions are affiliated to the Trades Union Congress (TUC), a policy-making body for the whole trade union movement which covers about 50 per cent of all workers. Its existence enables different unions to discuss and act on common issues, and it has sometimes negotiated with the government on overall pay rises and other national matters.

There are over 100 unions affiliated to the TUC, they include 'general' unions which cover a range of jobs – often unskilled – and specialist or 'craft' unions, covering specific trades.

Deciding which union to join is an important issue. If most of the workers in your workplace belong to one union, you are generally advised to join that one. If there are no members, or you have a choice, there are several ways of deciding: the TUC (26 Great Russell Street, London WC1, 071–636 4030) can advise you which unions are relevant to you. Contact them all and ask them to send you information. If there is a trade union resource centre, unemployed people's group or law centre in your area, they may have literature or views on the best unions locally. *The Trade Union Directory* (Pluto Press) lists all TUC unions and describes their policies.

If you join a trade union you have to pay 'dues', either directly to a union representative or by having them deducted from your wages. Some unions have reduced rates for young workers under 18 and contributions related to income. Membership costs will vary from union to union, ranging between a few pounds a year and over a hundred.

Unions will provide collective protection and negotiate for improved conditions, including pay. They will also represent you in any personal conflict you may have with your employer, appoint health and safety representatives, and represent you in tribunals. Union membership may also get you reductions in the price of holidays or of goods in some stores.

Union organisation

Terminology and practice vary from union to union. Generally you join a branch at your workplace or one which covers all members in your area. It should have regular meetings, at times and places that all members find convenient. Few, however, provide crèches for members with small children.

You elect your own representatives – often called shop stewards. In some unions they negotiate directly with the employer, in others they refer this to a local official who is paid by the union to work for you. Each branch has a branch committee, usually elected at an Annual General Meeting.

> 66
> **You have the legal right to join a trade union and to take part in its activities without victimisation.**
> 99

Unions have differing national structures, usually based on regional and divisional committees with a National Executive as the ultimate, policy-making body, or wth annual delegate meetings, to which the National Executive is answerable.

Unions are democratic, all representatives being elected, although the method of election may vary. As a member you can speak at meetings to try to affect policy, or put yourself up for office. But you are also bound by majority decisions, even if you do not agree with them.

Not all unions are recognised by employers. There is no legal right to recognition, so you will have to negotiate for it. In some workplaces there are 'closed shops'. This means that the employer and the union have agreed that all employees have to join the union, providing that the union has fulfilled certain legal requirements. However, these are likely soon to be made illegal, or if not will probably disappear anyway as both the Conservative and Labour Parties are now against them.

You have the legal right to join a trade union and to take part in its activities without victimisation. You also have a legal right, except in closed shops, not to join a union.

Industrial action

Since the 1982 Employment Act came into force, lawful industrial actions have been narrowed to those which relate 'wholly or mainly to trade disputes' such as those over pay and other conditions. Sympathetic action with other groups of workers will generally be illegal under this law. Employers can also now dismiss workers who have been on strike, provided that all the workers who took part in the strike are sacked and not re-employed.

Staff associations

Some workplaces have staff associations. These are often set up by employers to avoid their employees' joining trade unions. Being small and local they do not have the power of trade unions to negotiate for their membership nationally and are a bit more like a school council, with employers and workers represented. Employers usually have the final say. As a member of one, you will not have the same legal protection as a trade unionist when involved in activities related to your membership.

Maternity and paternity

If you become pregnant while you are working you have various statutory rights, but these are not very generous and you may find that the trade union at your workplace has negotiated better ones with your employer which both provide for higher payments and for longer periods.

Provided that you have worked for six months or more by the 26th week of your pregnancy for your employer, and your average weekly earnings have been above the Lower Earnings Limit (see p. 18) then you have the legal right to take maternity leave from the eleventh week before your baby is due up to 29 weeks after the birth. You are entitled then to your old job back, or suitable alternative employment if your job has been declared redundant or it is not reasonably practical for your employer to give you back exactly the same job. However, you don't have to return to the job afterwards if you don't want to.

It is actually illegal to work at some jobs if you are pregnant, usually because of possible harm to the baby, such as if you work with lead or radiation. In this case you have the right to alternative work if it is available; you can only be dismissed if it is not. In this case you are entitled to have your job back after the baby has been born.

The payment is determined by how long you have worked for your employer. If it is over two years at 16 hours a week or more, you get 90 per cent of your full pay for the first six weeks, then a lower rate of £36.25 (at the time of writing) thereafter. If you have worked for less time, or between eight and 16 hours a week, you get the lower rate throughout.

If you do not qualify for maternity pay you receive maternity allowance from the DSS (providing, as with other benefits you have paid the necessary number of National Insurance contributions) of £33.20 a week at the time of writing. This is paid for 13 weeks and you can start it between 11 to six weeks before the birth is due. If you do not qualify for maternity allowance you may get sickness benefit (see below).

Finally, you are legally entitled to paid time off to attend ante-natal check-ups, though your employer can ask for written proof of your pregnancy and the appointments before agreeing. You must also notify your employer 21 days before stopping work to get maternity pay.

There is no legal entitlement to time off during and after the birth if you are the father, but some unions have negotiated paternity agreements.

Childcare

If you have a child under school age you will probably have to make your own arrangements for his or her care while you are at work. It is rare for employers to provide workplace nurseries, but the numbers are now increasing, and some local authorities, colleges and hospitals have had them for several years.

The social services department of your local council can give you a list of approved childminders. They will charge around £15 to £30 a week, depending on the facilities and the number of other children being looked after by them.

Sexual harassment at work

Sexual harassment can be verbal pestering, touching or actual assault. It means more than the occasional banter that can be genuinely enjoyed by all those involved. In extreme cases it can lead to the loss of a job. Women (and it is almost invariably women who are the victims) who refuse advances from male superiors have actually been sacked, or forced to leave because life is made unbearable.

You don't have to put up with unwanted sexual advances at work. If you do find you are subjected to them, you should first of all ask the harasser to stop. If this doesn't work, then approach other women you trust for support, and approach your shop steward or the women's officer of your union branch. Keep a diary of incidents if they continue. Your union branch representative should press the employer to take disciplinary proceedings if harassment does not stop. If there is some reluctance to do this, possibly because the harasser is a fellow union member, contact the National Women's Officer of your union and/or organise yourself and other female colleagues and demand to be heard. You can get support from your local women's centre, and women's group, or contact the Rights For Women Unit at the National Council for Civil Liberties.

If the harasser is a superior and manages to dismiss you for not going along with him, then he could be breaking the Sex Discrimination Act, and you can apply to an industrial tribunal (see 'The Law' chapter). You could also argue that your employer is not providing a safe working environment and is breaking health and safety regulations!

29

Benefits while at work

Most of the benefits which you are entitled to as a worker are related to your National Insurance contributions. This means that first-time employees are not covered for a time, but your employer may anyway provide better terms than the legal ones. Providing you do qualify, the main benefits you may get are sick pay, sickness benefit, disablement benefit if permanently disabled, and family income supplement if you are on low pay and have children. You can also get income support in certain circumstances.

Statutory sick pay (SSP)

Statutory sick pay is generally paid for the first 28 weeks of sickness, provided you are earning more than £43 weekly and are employed. However, if you fell ill when out of work, before you started a job, have already drawn 28 weeks' sick pay in the current tax year, are on strike or on a short-term contract of less than three months, you will not be eligible.

Provided you are paying Class 1 contributions – even if you have just started work – you will be eligible for it. You should get your sick pay in with your wages. You must notify the employer within seven days of sickness that you intend to claim, and anyway should ring him or her as soon as possible on the first day to say you are ill. There are no rules governing the form your notification of sickness should take, but your employer is entitled to evidence he 'reasonably' needs to determine your SSP payment. A certificate from your doctor saying you are ill is not required during the first seven days of sickness.

What you get depends on your earnings. At the time of writing, it is £52.10 if you earn £84 a week or more and £36.25 if more than £43. You are not paid during the first three days of sickness, which are called 'waiting days'. You may find that your employer pays more than this – even full pay – in which case he or she probably will be claiming the sick pay from the DSS and topping it up.

Sickness benefit

Sickness benefit is paid to those not eligible for statutory sick pay, including people who have used up their allowance of sick pay. It is usually sent as a Giro cheque to your home. You must claim within six days of becoming ill and send a doctor's certificate.

The current rate is £33.20 weekly, irrespective of salary, with a dependant's allowance of £20.55. You can receive sickness benefit for 28 weeks in total, when you move on to invalidity benefits if you are still sick.

Invalidity benefits

If you have been entitled to sickness benefit, you should qualify for an invalidity pension, with an allowance for your spouse or other adult dependent and your children. At present a sick person gets £43.60 a week, with an extra payment based on earnings-related Class 1 NI contributions.

Industrial injury or disease

If you are off work due to an accident at work or 'prescribed' disease you can claim disablement benefit, even if you have not paid NI contributions. You should also notify your trade union at once, as you might have to demonstrate that your injury or illness was caused by your work. How much you get depends on the extent of your disablement, which is assessed on a percentage basis. If 100 per cent disabled you will receive £71.20 weekly, which is tax free and is in addition to your earnings.

Family Credit

Family Credit is designed to bring the income of employed people with families to a reasonable level. Simply, it is for the low paid. To get it you must live as a couple, have at least one child and be working for more than 24 hours a week. The amounts paid are determined by how much you earn, how many children you have and how old they are. For example, you could be earning £80 a week and have a four-year-old child and receive over £23 per week Family Credit. If you think you are eligible, get an application form from a post office or social security office.

Income support

Income support is not usually available for employed people, but it can be paid if you work part-time, are a single parent, are looking after a sick dependant or are registered as a blind person. Apply to your local Social Security office.

Redundancy, dismissal and notice

You might not want to start thinking about these as you enter a job, but they are crucial areas of law to understand. They are also very complex and it is only possible to give a summary here. For more information you should consult your union, a law centre, the Citizens Advice Bureau, or the publications listed at the back of this book.

Notice

When you start a job the length of notice of your departure you will have to give your employer will be agreed in your terms of employment. It may be a week, a month or three months. If you want to leave your job for any reason, give your employer a letter stating your intention to leave when that time has elapsed. It's polite to explain in the letter why you are leaving – assuming it's not just because you hate the place – and in any event bear in mind that a future potential employer might contact the one you are now leaving for an opinion of you.

> **66**
>
> **If you want to leave your job for any reason, give your employer a letter stating your intention.**
>
> **99**

When you go you will be given a P45, which is a form stating your tax position, which you need for your next employer, or the unemployment office.

Redundancy

Redundancy occurs when a business is going to cease trading or when the employer considers that the need for work of a particular kind no longer exists.

If you are subject to redundancy, you have some legal rights. You are entitled to redundancy pay, depending on the length of your service and age. You cannot be unfairly chosen for redundancy – for example you cannot be singled out because you are active in the union, or just because you are a part-time worker. You have to be given notice of redundancy, the length of notice being the same as your entitlement under any kind of dismissal. You also have the right to reasonable time off without pay to look for a job.

The right of redundancy pay is restricted. Workers are not eligible at all until the age of 20, and nobody is entitled unless they have worked for the same employer for at least two years (five years if working less than 16 hours and more than eight hours a week).

The pay is half a week's pay for each year of service if you are under 22, more if you are older. However, some employers pay more, and even if there is no pre-existing agreement your trade union, if you are covered by one, will try to negotiate better terms once impending redundancies have been announced.

Your employer may offer you alternative work rather than make you redundant. It must be the same or 'not substantially different', and suitable for you, and you have the right to four weeks' trial to decide whether it is. If before the four weeks are up you realise that the work is not suitable you are entitled to the redundancy and the redundancy pay.

You cannot be temporarily laid-off without pay, unless your contract allows for it. If you have been laid off for four or more weeks you will be able to leave and claim redundancy.

Dismissal

You can be dismissed from your job if your employer considers that you are not doing it properly or your conduct is poor. However, you cannot be dismissed for trade union activity.

If your employer wishes to dismiss you he or she also has to give notice. There are minimum periods specified by law: one week if you have worked for him or her for more than a month and less than two years, and one week for each year of service after that, up to a maximum of twelve weeks. Again, these are minimum periods, and you may have better terms.

If you consider that your dismissal is unfair, take it up immediately with your trade union representative. If you do not have one, or if the union cannot get the employer to change his or her mind, then you can take the employer to an industrial tribunal (see 'The Law' chapter). You must apply within 13 weeks, and you must have worked for your employer for two years. If the tribunal agrees that you have been dismissed unfairly it can insist that your employer gives you your job back, or, more usually, that he or she pays you compensation.

S ELF-EMPLOYMENT

Working for yourself and being your own boss can be attractive as it means you have much more control over your working life than you get working for someone else. But it can also mean a lot of hard work and long hours, and there is no guarantee that you will make enough money to live on. Becoming self-employed involves careful planning, but that doesn't mean you should be put off.

First of all think about what type of work you want to do. There are basically four different ways to be self-employed – piece work, homeworking, working freelance, and starting your own business.

Then consider these questions: Have you got a good idea? Do you know exactly what is involved in terms of time, work and money? Is there a need for this work in your area? Do you have all the skills or experience you need, or do you need some more training? Will you know where to go for help?

If you are still interested there are plenty of useful organisations to talk to. Don't be frightened to go to them and discuss your ideas. They can give you expert advice on all aspects of becoming self-employed or starting a business, usually for free.

Piece work

Piece work means you are paid for each particular job you do. For example, you may set yourself up as a car-sprayer and get paid for each car you spray, or you make electrical circuits or assemble jewellery, and be paid per finished item. In the latter instances you will be producing the work for someone else to sell; if you are selling it yourself you will probably be running your own business.

Before you decide to take up piece work, it is important to find out the going rate for each job, and how long the work will take you. Make sure that it is not going to take you a long time to do in relation to the payment; as you will be working for a fixed rate and not by the hour, you could find that a long job is not economical. This applies to each job you take on: make sure that the payment is agreed in advance and do a careful calculation of how long it will take you.

As a piece worker you will usually be defined for tax and National Insurance purposes as self-employed, but you might be a 'service only sub-contractor'. This is the case when someone else provides you with all or most of your work but you are not their employee, and you are paying your own tax and National Insurance contributions, for example if you are spraying cars but all the work is provided by the same garage owner.

Look in your local papers or Jobcentre for piece work as it is often advertised there. However, watch out for adverts which say you can earn lots of money. It may sound good but the example quoted may be of someone who has worked at the job for a long time and can do it quickly.

Homeworking

Homeworking means work that you do at home! Most homeworking is a form of piece work, but the homeworker will only work from home, while the piece worker may work at someone else's place of work. Usually the work will be brought to you; it is convenient if you have a baby or small child to look after or you cannot leave the house because you are disabled. You will almost be certainly be classified as self-employed.

Homeworking is varied and sometimes involves unusual kinds of work. It is usually one of two types: making things, such as knitting, sewing, making jewellery or lampshades, or providing a service, such as typing, addressing envelopes, childcare, answering the telephone or computer programming.

The trouble with homeworking is that the pay can be very low, so make sure you know exactly how much you will be paid. You might be paid by the hour or by what you produce – for example, by the page if you are typing. Make sure that you won't have to work all day and night just to make a living. And watch out for firms that ask you to pay money for materials or equipment before you get any work. Don't pay; if you do you may find that you don't get any work, or if you do get work, the pay may be so low that you are not able to cover your original costs.

While you may have the advantages of being at home and being your own boss, as a homeworker you have to pay your own heating and lighting bills as well as tax and National Insurance and the work may be irregular.

There are various organisations which will help you, especially the Low Pay Unit, 9 Upper Berkeley Street, London, W1 (071-262 7278). You could also contact the local Wages Inspectorate, as they cover some types of homework.

Freelancing

Working freelance means that you sell a service to people and get paid for it, such as photography, graphic design, journalism or computer programming. Most freelances have acquired their skill by working first as an employee for a company.

Usually you will spend short amounts of time with different companies, working either at the company or at home. For instance, if a company needs a particular computer program but doesn't have anyone on the staff who can write it, it may ask a freelance computer programmer to do the job. The programmer will not be an employee of the company but will be paid a fee for that particular assignment. Quite a lot of journalism is done by freelances, who either will be commissioned by newspapers and magazines to write specific articles, or will submit articles they have already written.

If you think there is a need for your service consider whether you will need any equipment and how much it will cost, whether you have all the skills you need, how much it will cost you to provide the service and whether there is a going rate for it, and how much you will have to do to make good money. Some jobs may be one-off or only busy at certain times of the year, so make sure you will be able to manage if the work isn't regular. Freelance work also usually involves travelling to different places so you may need transport.

66

Most freelances have acquired their skill by working first as an employee.

99

Your local business advice centre may be able to help you and advise you of any grants to help you get started.

Starting a business

Starting a business can be a big step, but it is possible to start in a small way and without much money. Running a business means that you will have to take all the initiatives and responsibility. You will have to make all the arrangements for buying stock, carrying out the work, and selling it.

Before you begin, it is a good idea to visit an advice centre to discuss your ideas and find out what sort of help is available. Most towns have some sort of agency which gives advice to people who want to set up small businesses. They will have a name such as Business Promotion Centre or Small Firms Service. Local Chambers of Commerce can also help.

The Small Firms Service is there to help and advise people on all aspects of setting up a business; to contact them ring the operator and ask for Freefone 2444. There is a Welsh branch, the Welsh Development Agency (044–385 2666) and a Scottish branch in the Scottish Development Agency (031–337 9595). In Northern Ireland contact the local Enterprise Development Unit (0232–691031).

The Young Enterprise scheme also offers advice. It organises groups with advisers from the world of business, setting up simulated situations such as you will encounter in running a business. It does not lend money, but aims to prepare you for the practical problems involved in setting up and running a business.

There are different types of business you can set up. If you are on your own you are known as a 'sole trader'. If your business is with another person it is officially called a 'partnership'. A 'limited company' has shareholders and directors, and they do not have financial liability if the business goes bust other than what they have invested in it. Finally, there are 'co-operatives' where everyone has an equal say in what happens: they have to have a minimum of seven partners. More information on co-operatives can be obtained from the Co-operative Development Agency, Broadmead House, 21 Panton Street, London SW1Y 4DR (071–839 2985).

For some types of work, such as market stall or a take-away food shop, you may need a licence from your local council. Check at a Citizens Advice Bureau if you think this might apply to you.

Finance

Some businesses, such as gardening and cleaning, don't require much investment, but many do. You may need to buy stock or machinery, and you might need separate premises. (If you plan to work from home check that your tenancy agreement or deeds allow you to run a business there.) You are also more likely to need some sort of insurance – for a car or van, to cover against an accident to stock or equipment, to cover you against an accident or long illness, and to cover employees or customers against accidents. If your business brings you into contact with customers' property, consider insuring against damage to that too – for example, breaking a valuable vase in a house you are cleaning.

There are many ways you can borrow money (see 'Money

Matters' chapter), but it is not easy if you are young and you will have to work hard to persuade people to lend it to you because they need to know that you will eventually be able to pay it back.

It helps if you can show some well-prepared figures. Business Advice Centres will help you work out what you need (addresses from Jobcentres, local councils or Citizens Advice Bureaux).

Grants

Certain areas can give special grants to people setting up businesses – usually where there is high unemployment. A Business Advice Centre will be able to tell you if you are eligible.

The government also runs the Enterprise Allowance Scheme to help unemployed people start their own business. Under it you get £40 per week for up to one year. It is taxable and is paid every two weeks straight into your bank account. In order to qualify you must have been unemployed for 8 weeks and be getting unemployment benefit or income support. You also have to be 18 or over, and have to have at least £1,000 to use in the business. Money borrowed, say from a bank, will count. You will have to open a special bank account for the business.

To apply for the allowance go to your local Jobcentre who will require you to attend an information session arranged by them before giving you an application form.

Tax, National Insurance and benefits

If you are self-employed you have to pay your own tax and National Insurance contributions out of any money you make. You must keep a clear record of your business finances as the Inland Revenue needs to see details of your financial affairs to work out how much tax you have to pay. You can claim allowances which mean you pay less tax (see p. 98), but this can get quite complicated. There may be courses run locally to help you learn how to keep proper accounts. Ask around at local colleges and the Business Advice Centre.

It may be a good idea to employ an accountant either to keep your records for you or to help you with your tax, as he or she will be able to advise you on which allowances to claim. Accountants are expensive but can easily save you more money than they cost. Ask people you know in the same sort of work as you for the names of good accountants who will understand your business. Alternatively, a Business Advice Centre may suggest one that deals with small businesses.

For National Insurance you pay Class 2 contributions. You can either get a stamp card from the DSS through their local social security office and buy stamps each week at a post office, or pay by direct debit through your bank, if you have a bank account. Contributions for the self-employed are £4.25 a week at the time of writing. If you can't afford this because your earnings are low, you may be allowed to pay less.

Before starting, contact your local social security for leaflet N141: 'A Guide to National Insurance for the Self-employed'.

> **66**
>
> **Accountants are expensive but can easily save you much more money than they cost.**
>
> **99**

If you are not earning much money when you start off in business you may be able to get supplementary benefit, although it is unlikely because you have to show that you are available for work and if you are spending most of your time trying to get your business going, then you probably won't qualify. But if in doubt, claim, and tell the DSS how much time you spend working. If you don't qualify, they will soon tell you.

If you can't work because you are sick you may be able to claim sickness benefit. You may not qualify because you have to have paid a certain number of National Insurance contributions. But if you don't get sickness benefit and you have little or no money coming in from the business, then you can claim income support (see next chapter).

U̲NEMPLOYMENT

With a volatile jobs market and a high rate of unemployment far more people than used to be the case have to face the grim fact that they may go on the dole at some time in their working lives. Being unemployed can be miserable and lonely, but it need not be, and there are lots of ways to fill in your time usefully. Many of these can, in fact, lead to getting a job. One thing you must do right away is to work out what your benefits should be.

Registering as unemployed

If you have not found work or are not continuing your full-time education after you leave school, you are guaranteed a place on a YTS scheme (see p. 50), providing you are under 18. You are not eligible for unemployment benefit or, normally, for income support.

If you are over 18 and have lost your job, or have left school or college with no job to go to, you will have to register as unemployed ('sign on'). There are two reasons why you must do this: first, the careers office can help you to find work, and second, you have to register to get money from the Department of Social Security.

Unfortunately, you won't be able to sign on for money as soon as you leave school as you are not entitled to it in the holiday following your last term. Normally you will have to wait until the beginning of the next school term, which means if you leave at Christmas you wait until the first working Monday in January; if you leave at Easter it will be the first Monday after Easter Monday; and if you leave in June, the first Monday in September. However, if you are 19 before the first Monday in September you can sign on on the Monday before your nine-teenth birthday, and if you are already 19 when you leave school you can sign on straight away. Note also that these waiting times don't apply if you are:

- an orphan or have left home and are estranged from family or guardian, but not in care
- if you have a child
- if you are severely disabled.

Ask at the DSS if you think you fit into any of these categories.

If you are 18 or under you have to go to your local careers office or Jobcentre to register for a YTS place. The careers centre will have details of YTS opportunities in your area.

Claiming benefit

Unemployment benefit, commonly called the 'dole', is only paid to people who have worked and made the necessary number of National Insurance contributions. Unless you have paid enough contributions by working in your holidays, you will not be eligible for it, but the rules say that you must still apply! You will usually get income support instead, which is paid to all sorts of people whose income or other benefits aren't enough or who don't have any income at all.

You will probably be asked to fill in the form for unemploy-ment benefit in the unemployment benefit office, but you may be able to take it away with you. Ask for a special envelope, if you haven't been given one, fill in the form as soon as possible and send it to the DSS. Your claim will be dealt with as soon as possible, but it will take time.

In either case, if you have not worked yet you will get a letter stating that you are not eligible for unemployment benefit. But don't panic, you may still get income support.

'Signing on'

After you have registered as unemployed and have been to the unemployment benefit office, you will be given a time to 'sign on'. The time and day will be written on a card called a UB40 which is proof that you are unemployed and available for work. Usually you will have to go back to the unemployment benefits office to sign on at that time specified once every two weeks, but you can be asked to do so weekly.

Once you have started signing on regularly you should get your benefit – whether it's unemployment benefit or income support, or both – by post in the form of a giro two days after each signing-on. You cash your giro at the post office where you will have to produce some proof of identification, such as your birth certificate or medical card. (There is a list at your post office giving other ways of identifying yourself.)

Income support

As an unemployed school-leaver income support is likely to be your main source of money if you are 18 or over.

To be able to claim income support you must normally live in this country, not be in full-time education, not have savings of £6000 or more, not work 24 hours or more a week, nor have a partner who works 24 hours a week or more. That's the easy part!

Calculating how much you will get is more difficult. There are strict rules about how it is worked out and the amounts are set by the government each year. What you receive is calculated according to how much the rules say you need to live on, the needs of any partner and/or children and any special needs of your own, housing costs, any savings you may have over £3000 and any income from other sources such as part-time work or other benefits.

> 66
>
> **All those who leave school under 18 and who do not have a job are guaranteed a paid place on a Youth Training Scheme.**
>
> 99

The basic allowances at the time of writing are £41.60 for a couple if both under 18 and £54.80 if one or both of them is over 18, £27.40 for single people aged 18–24, and £34.90 for single people aged 18–24 bringing up a child on their own. In addition you get £11.75 for each child under 11. This is what the DSS assumes you need to cover food, heating and clothing.

The DSS then looks at any special requirements that are particular to you. For example, you may be disabled, a single parent, or the parent of a disabled child. Further allowances go into the calculations for these, known as premiums. If you have any of these, or any additional requirements, make sure you claim for them, and if in doubt seek advice from your social security office or an advice centre such as the Citizens Advice Bureau. The form on which you apply for income support is designed to find out details of your personal situation so as to establish whether you are eligible for premium payments.

Finally, if you get income support you are also entitled to housing benefit to cover your rent or accommodation costs, and if you have a mortgage you can get additional income support payments to pay the interest. You also get the maximum rebate of 80 per cent of the community charge (see p.101); the other 20 per cent is supposed to be covered by your personal allowance.

The DSS now adds up your personal allowance, any benefits and housing costs and deducts from this your income. The income is both what you and your partner earn after deduction of tax, National Insurance, half of any pension contributions and £5 for each person working, plus any benefits you receive, plus interest on any savings over £3000. The sum left after this bit of arithmetic is what you receive.

There are a few cases when you can also get income support if you are over 16 but under 18. These are if you are on YTS with a dependant partner or child and the training allowance is not enough to support them, or if you are a single parent, disabled, an orphan with no-one looking after you, or if you are not living with your parents or being supported by them.

To get income support apply at your local security office. They can give you a form, SB1, which tells you more about it.

If you think that you are not getting everything you are entitled to, take it up with your local social security office, and if you are still not satisfied, go to an advice centre. However, if you are getting the correct amount but it is too low for you to manage on, there isn't very much you can do other than contact your MP and complain.

Social Fund

If you are on income support you may be eligible for one-off payments or loans to cover specific requirements. These are paid out of the Social Fund, which is a scheme that was introduced in 1988 to replace the previous system of single payments.

There is a whole range of these payments, with different rules for each. Some of them are at the discretion of the social security office and come from a limited budget, which means that however good your case may be, you may not receive the payment simply because the money isn't there. An example of these is community care grants, which are designed to help people improve their housing if this would prevent them otherwise going into residential care, or to help with a family problem such as the breakdown of a marriage.

Some other payments are made as loans. These are to cover

such things as buying furniture or a cooker, making essential house repairs, or dealing with the aftermath of a burglary or a fire. There is no right to these loans, and you may be refused if the social security officer handling your application considers that you might not be able to pay the loan back. This means, of course, that the more you are in need of the loan, the less likely you are to be given it!

Those on income support are entitled to receive a grant if they have a new baby. This is not repayable, nor discretionary, and at the time of writing is fixed at £85.

To apply for a payment under the Social Fund you make a claim through the local social security office, who will give you a form to fill in. If it is for a crisis payment, such as the aftermath of a burglary or fire, you will have to have an interview with a social security officer.

Apart from the maternity payment there is no right of appeal against any decision on loans or grants. If you are unhappy with the response you get to your claim you can merely ask the DSS to reconsider, and if the repayment terms for a loan strike you as unfair you can complain but you are not guaranteed any hearing.

Unemployment benefit

You are entitled to unemployment benefit if you are unemployed and actively looking for work and have paid enough National Insurance (NI) contributions at the right time (see p. 18). Unemployment benefit is paid for 312 days (one year not counting Sundays), and unlike supplementary benefit is a single fixed amount – at the time of writing £34.70 per week.

You may be able to get income support as well as unemployment benefit, depending on your situation. Unemployment benefit counts as income when working out your income support entitlement. If you are unemployed and have your own place you are probably entitled to housing benefit (see p. 167).

You can claim unemployment benefit while working, provided that you don't earn more than £2 per day and are still available for work. Unemployment benefit is, in fact, paid for each day that you are unemployed, so even if you work on one day, say a Saturday job, and earn more than £2, you will just lose benefit for that day; however much you have earned it will not affect your entitlement for the rest of the week. However, if you work for a couple of days a week or more you could run into problems, as there is a rule meant to stop people earning money for a few days each week and claiming unemployment benefit for the rest. If your benefit is stopped because of this rule, and you think it has been done so unfairly, you can appeal, but you must do so in writing to the benefit office within 28 days.

Because unemployment benefit isn't paid to you for Sundays, any money you earn on Sundays does not affect your benefit at all. So you can earn as much as you like then, and still get the full amount for the rest of the week. However you should tell the unemployment benefit office if you are doing this.

Looking for a job

Although you may have tried many avenues for getting a job, there may be others which you have not considered. In any event a job is not likely to jump up and offer itself to you; it's up to you to keep yourself in the running and exploit as many opportunities as possible.

The local careers office should help you to work out some of your own ideas about what you want to do, if you have not already done so. You will have to see them to register as unemployed, but you can also make appointments at other times. They'll be able to put you into contact with colleges, workshops, schemes and possible employers.

Jobcentres have details of jobs available in their area, and you can go in whenever you like to see what jobs they have. They get to hear of new jobs every day, so go in regularly. The staff there can also give advice on looking for work in other areas. Use the local press. Most newspapers run a 'situations vacant' section, so it's worth getting hold of the nationals and locals as soon as they come out. That doesn't mean you've got to buy them as the local library will keep them all in their reading room, as will the local unemployment or drop-in centre if you've got one in your area.

Why not put in an ad yourself, in the 'Situations Wanted' section, stating what you can do and what you're interested in? Make it sound appealing – remember, you are actually trying to sell yourself.

Find out if your local radio station runs a job-finding service, and if so get into the habit of tuning in. If they don't, ask why not, and suggest they start one up. And don't forget the trade press, magazines and newspapers that specialise in certain job areas.

Employment agencies are private companies that try to find the right person for the job for firms or companies that pay them to do so. They are particularly useful for office, catering and shop work. If you haven't got any particular skill you only have a slim chance of them finding work for you, but their service is free, so it's worth a try. There is at least one in most high streets.

Local shop windows, and even some factories, often display vacant positions. Walk around and have a look; consider putting an ad in a window yourself. Visiting companies, factories and businesses that you are interested in and then selling your services can be effective; at least it shows your enthusiasm.

The saying 'It's not what you know but who' is actually quite true when looking for a job. Let friends, relatives and neighbours know you're looking for work, and ask them to keep their ears open.

Use the services of people specifically employed to help you: the area youth officer, youth club workers, community services workers. They often hear about work opportunities before anybody else, and they'll especially be able to advise you if you're disabled or have been in trouble with the police. Have a browse through some books next time you're in the library. *Facing Unemployment* and *The Unemployment Handbook* are full of ideas for using your time. *Occupations '90* is held at the

Jobcentre. Some books will carry ads for firms that have regular recruitment drives, like the post office and banks.

The Youth Training Scheme (YTS)

You will probably have heard of the Youth Training Scheme during your last year at school. If you cannot find work and are under 18 you are guaranteed a place on it. The scheme is a two-year programme, providing at least 20 weeks off-the-job training and some sort of qualification at the end. You are not obliged to take up the place offered, but if you do not you will not be able to claim unemployment benefit or income support.

The YTS is now run by the Training Agency and was started under the auspices of the Manpower Services Agency to provide training and work experience for school-leavers. Although the Agency is responsible for YTS is does not run every scheme from day to day. This is usually done by 'agents' or 'sponsors', who are employers, colleges, local councils, or voluntary groups. Or a scheme could be run by more than one of these groups working together, such as a building firm with one day a week at a local college.

You are guaranteed a place on YTS if you are 16 and have left school without a job to go to. If it is less than a year since you left school, you should get a place for two years on YTS. But if it is more than a year since you left school, you may only be guaranteed a place for one year.

If you think that you are not covered by any of these criteria ask at the careers office or Jobcentre as you may still be able to get a place.

Your local careers office will have most information about schemes in your area. Jobcentres and employment offices may also be able to help so they could be worth a visit. Some employers who run YTS schemes take people on directly instead of going through the Jobcentre or careers office so it is worth looking in local newspapers for adverts to see if there is anything that appeals to you.

Trainees and employees

If you are on a YTS scheme, you will be either a trainee or an employee. As a trainee you receive a weekly allowance of £29.50 during the first year and £35.00 during the second if you are on a two-year scheme; on a one-year scheme you get £29.50 for the first 13 weeks, then £35. Some employers pay more than the training allowance but this is unusual. If you are paid more than the allowance then you are likely to be an employee instead of a trainee, and this determines your employment rights. As a trainee you may not have a contract of employment or pay tax or National Insurance, but as an employee you may have to pay both, depending on how much extra you get, and you should have a contract.

Conditions of employment

Apart from tax and your entitlement to a contract, your status affects other aspects of YTS. YTS employees should have the same employment rights as other employees (see 'Employment' chapter). As a general rule, trainees should not work more than 40 hours per week, not including any breaks for meals or tea. There may be local rules which affect your hours. If you are having problems ask the Training Agency.

YTS employees should have the same employment rights as other employees.

Trainees should get 1½ days holiday for each month you work and you should be paid during your holidays and all normal bank and public holidays. However, you can only take holidays during your time on YTS. When you leave you will not get holiday pay for any holidays you have not taken, so make sure you take all of your holiday entitlement while you are on the scheme.

At present, trainees are also entitled to the extra cost of travel if it costs more than £4.00 a week for them to get to work.

If you are a trainee no statutory sick pay will be paid if you are off sick. However, your normal allowance will be paid for up to three weeks of illness each year, but you must have followed your scheme's rules about telling your supervisor that you are sick. Make sure you know what these rules are when you start your scheme or you may lose out on part of your money. If you are off for seven days or less you can fill in your own sick note. But if you are off for eight days or more you must get a note from your doctor to send to your supervisor. If you are off sick for three weeks or longer you may lose your place, but should be allowed to join another scheme when you are well again.

Trainees are not currently covered by the main rules of the Health and Safety at Work Act but employers must make sure that they or their health are not in danger. YTS trainees who work in a factory are, however, covered by the rules of the Factories Act. If you are worried about health and safety on YTS you should first talk to your supervisor, but if the company does not give you a satisfactory answer you can take it up with someone from the local Health and Safety Executive or someone from the local Environmental Health department (this could be under the name of the local council in the phone book, if it's not under Environmental Health). Alternatively, if you are a member of a trade union – and YTS trainees are entitled to join unions – ask your trade union representative.

If you are involved in an industrial accident, report it right away. If you think you have a claim, ask for legal advice, or go to your trade union. Some Citizens Advice Bureaux and law centres can also arrange for you to see a solicitor. However, only employees can claim an industrial disablement benefit for an accident at work which results in you being hurt, or for a disease contracted because of the nature of the work. Trainees should be compensated by the Training Agency for the same amount as they would otherwise get from the DSS. If this happens to you, contact the Agency immediately.

As a trainee you should be allowed time off to go to interviews for jobs or for a place on another training course. You will not lose any pay if you give your supervisor or scheme manager adequate warning that you may need time off. If you are an employee on YTS you do not have a right to time off, and it is up to your employer to decide whether he or she gives it to you. You can, of course, take it as holiday.

If you are a trainee and take time off without permission then you may lose some of your pay. If this happens to you and you feel that it is unfair, you can always challenge the decision, by discussing it with your supervisor or scheme manager.

Grievance procedures

If you have a problem at work or there is something you're not happy with, you can discuss it with the management and try to clear it up. Most problems are settled reasonably amicably with the direct supervisor, but if you need to go further, there may be certain rules you have to follow to try and sort your problem out – this is called a 'grievance procedure'.

You should be told what the grievance procedure is when you first start on your scheme. If there are no clear rules, you should start by talking to your supervisor. If the supervisor can't help then go to the scheme manager. At this stage you can take someone with you. You may like someone to put your problem to the manager for you, such as your mother or father, a trade union representative, or an advice worker.

If you have a serious problem that can't be sorted out this way then go to the careers office or nearest Training Agency. They will help you. If you do decide to contact either of these you should tell the scheme management that you are going to do so.

Discipline and dismissal

Although you're not costing your employer in wages, nevertheless he will expect punctuality, civility and a certain amount of effort. If you do not measure up or do something which is against your scheme rules then disciplinary action may be taken against you. This could mean losing some of your pay, being suspended or sacked. The person or organisation who runs your scheme will decide on what the disciplinary action should be and when it should be used.

The Training Agency does suggest to employers and scheme organisers that you should be given a chance to put your side of what has happened, and if you want to you can have someone to put your case to the management for you. The Agency also suggests that you should be given warnings before you are suspended or sacked and that you should be able to appeal if you think that action taken against you has been unfair. Sometimes schemes do not follow these suggestions, and unfortunately there isn't very much you can do about it.

If the organisation does want to sack you, as a trainee you are not entitled to a period of notice or written reasons for the dismissal. You cannot claim unfair dismissal to an Industrial Tribunal either. Employees, on the other hand, do have these rights as long as they have worked for the right length of time. But if, as a trainee, you feel you have been treated badly, you should talk to your scheme manager and ask him or her to explain why you have been dismissed. If you are not happy with this explanation then contact the nearest Training Agency or careers office.

If you are dismissed you are still entitled to be paid for any periods of time which you have already worked.

After being dismissed you should sign on straight away. There is no law that says your supplementary benefit should in any way be affected because you were dismissed. You may be able to join another YTS scheme, but you will only be able to do it for two years, less the time you have spent on the first one.

Leaving YTS

If you already have a YTS place you may be able to transfer to another scheme, if the Training Agency thinks that your present scheme is not right for you. But if you have lost your YTS place because of illness or some other reason which was not your fault, the Agency has to find you a place on another scheme. However, you don't have to stay the full two years, nor do you have to give any notice if you are a trainee, but it's polite to do so. If you leave without a good reason, you will not receive any benefit.

At the end of your scheme you get a YTS certificate, even if you did not stay for the full two years. This says what skills, knowledge and experience you have gained during the time you have spent on the scheme.

Employment Training

The Employment Training scheme (ET) was set up in the late 1980s to provide training opportunities for the unemployed. To qualify you have to be over 18 and to have been out of work for at least six months.

The principle behind ET is to give the unemployed skills which will not only give them a better chance of finding a job, but the chance of finding a better job than they might otherwise have done. If you decide to go on the scheme you initially talk to a training agent who helps draw up a training plan to match your interests and the opportunities. The subsequent training involves working with an employer, and possibly some time on a project. It may also involve time at a college or other training centre.

While you are on the scheme you receive your full benefits, plus £10 a week training allowance. In addition you are reimbursed any travel costs over £4 a week, and are entitled to child care costs if you are a single parent.

The scheme lasts for a year, but you can leave at any time before then if you are offered a job. Your local Jobcentre will have details.

Other forms of work

Although they are not careers, and may not be paid at all, there are other forms of work you can do. At worst, they are better than staying at home and staring at the wall, while they can be stimulating and rewarding and even lead to something else.

Temporary and casual work

There isn't always much temporary or casual work about, but it does turn up. So keep a look out in local papers and the Jobcentre, and ask around.

The work may not last long, and can play havoc with your benefits, but on the other hand you do earn some money and you make more contacts with employers. These might produce a reference for a full-time job, and will always give you work experience. You are officially allowed to earn £5 a week without it affecting the amount of income support you get, and that's after expenses such as bus fares and the cost of materials. It may not seem like a lot, but if you do take an almost unpaid job it's better than nothing, and there's always the chance that what you do to earn that extra cash could lead to bigger things.

There are quite a lot of summer jobs of all sorts, and *Summer Jobs Abroad*, edited by David Woodworth and *Summer Jobs in Britain*, edited by David Stephens are worth examining. Both are published by Vacation Work. They are full of jobs; check the pay recorded and see if the job includes accommodation.

Be careful of adverts in the local paper which claim to make you lots of money quickly. They are usually jobs which involve selling things from door-to-door. You may like to try them but check how much you will be paid, and whether it depends on how much you sell, and find out about the company first if you are asked to hand over any money.

Voluntary work

Voluntary work comes in an almost endless variety of forms – from being an advice worker in a Citizens Advice Bureau or law centre, to decorating or gardening for the elderly, helping people to read and write, or working in a play group. While you don't get paid – so it doesn't usually affect your benefits – you do usually get travel expenses and cheap or free coffee and tea.

You also get to keep warm, without using your own fuel. Above all, you make lots of useful contacts, people who hear about jobs, and get a reference if you are applying for jobs. Potential employers like to know what you've been doing with your time, so you have something positive to put on application forms and to talk about at interviews. Voluntary jobs provide experience in different types of work, and you also get to meet new friends. Finally, this kind of work usually has a social purpose, and you may well enjoy feeling useful.

Most towns have some voluntary groups. To find out what's around try the library, the Tourist Information Centre (where there are lots of posters), Community Service Volunteers, the Community Council, the Voluntary Projects Programme, the Volunteer Bureau or the Citizens Advice Bureau.

The National Association of Youth Clubs runs some special projects for young people, in addition to their youth clubs. These include Community Industry, which offers paid voluntary work for young people from disadvantaged backgrounds, and Practical Action, which provides young people with equipment and services from industry and commerce.

If you are claiming while doing voluntary work, you must show that you're still available should a job come up. If you are involved in work locally, that's not a problem, but if you go on a summer camp for more than two weeks, or become involved in long-term work, you won't be eligible for benefit. However, longer-term schemes will pay you board and lodgings and give you some pocket money.

Moonlighting

Some people take on 'moonlighting', which means working and not telling the DSS about it.

Each time you sign on you are signing a statement that your situation hasn't changed since you last signed on. You say you are still unemployed and available for work, and that's why you get your money. So if you are earning money from work it will affect how much benefit you get. If you do not declare your earnings, it is illegal and you are liable to be fined and certainly to pay back the benefit that shouldn't have been claimed.

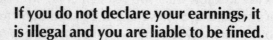

If you do not declare your earnings, it is illegal and you are liable to be fined.

Some people feel that moonlighting enables them to make good contacts for regular work if it comes along. But it should be borne in mind that employers who take on casual workers may not be in a position to take on workers permanently. While having a job could give you confidence, with this kind of work you never know who your friends are. And if the DSS receive a report or even just a 'phone call about you they have to look into it. It's possible that you could be prosecuted.

Studying while unemployed

One way of avoiding unemployment is to carry on your education at a sixth form college (if you're 16 to 19), technical college or night school (see the next chapter). But you may not want to go to these lengths and in many larger towns there are special study courses for unemployed people, which may include subjects and skills training that aren't available in schools. Even if there aren't special courses it is well worth looking at what's on offer at evening and day classes. If you are getting benefit, you won't usually have to pay any fees.

Apart from developing a skill, or just extending an interest, part-time study gives you contact with other people, and something to look forward to each week. Moreover, any courses you take will provide you with extra information to put on application forms for jobs. Even if the course isn't particularly relevant to the job, employers like to see that you have been trying to use your free time usefully and productively – it shows them that you have initiative.

Benefits during study

If you are 16, 17 or 18 you cannot usually claim income support while you are at school or college, nor can you if you take on a part-time course while looking for work. Your parents may, however, be able to claim child benefit.

There are some exceptions. You are eligible for income support if you are a parent with your children living with you, are disabled and not likely to get a job in the next year, are an orphan with no one who is acting as your parent, or are living away from home, have no contact at all with your parents, and do not live with anyone else who is acting as your parent.

Certain people over 18 may claim income support while studying. These are those who come under the 21 Hour Rule. To be able to claim under this you have to be doing a course of 21 hours' tuition a week or less (not including homework), and you must be prepared to give it up if a suitable job turns up. You also have to have been on income support, or a Youth Training Scheme for three months before the course starts, or during three out of the last six months and have been working for the rest of the time. If you leave school in the summer you probably won't be able to claim under the 21 Hour Rule because you will not meet the three-month qualification.

To get the benefit you have to convince the DSS that you are still available for work. This could be difficult. They will look at how long your course is and whether it is called part-time by the college or education authority. You may need help from your local advice centre or college, which may be able to tell you about similar cases and how the DSS have treated the claims.

If you have been refused income support because you are studying you can appeal, but must do so in writing within 28 days.

Filling your time

If you are completely unemployed you won't have much money, but you will have plenty of time. It's easy to waste time when you're unemployed, but there are lots of things you can do to try to keep active (see also 'Using your time' chapter).

At some time you will probably feel down or depressed and although you may not be able to avoid these feelings, it does help if you can keep busy and make yourself do something. If you are feeling isolated or lonely, try and involve yourself in some activity on a regular basis, even if it's only going round to see a friend or down the road for a drink once a week. Talking to other people who are in the same position may help.

On days when you feel depressed try to remember that you won't always feel so bad, and keep in touch with other people, as there's nothing worse than being depressed on your own. If you've got an activity to go to, then you can keep in contact with other people and have an incentive to do something.

Centres for the unemployed

If you live in a medium-sized town, the chances are that there will be some sort of centre or club for unemployed people. They may be run by voluntary groups such as churches or the YMCA, by trade unions, by social services or by a group of unemployed people who have decided to get together.

Activities at these centres can involve just getting together for a chat and a drink (at below pub prices), but they will probably also include welfare benefits sessions, sports, free entertainment and benefit campaigns. They are generally friendly and welcoming, and will help with problems as much as they can. If you are interested in finding a centre near you, ask at the local Information Centre (or Tourist Information Centre), Citizens Advice Bureau, or library.

Using your UB40

Your UB40 or 'signing-on' card can be very useful if you're short of money. In some places where there are lots of people who are unemployed, the UB40 can be used as a way of doing things cheaply. For example, it can get reduced-price admission into theatres, cinemas and concerts, and cheap or free use of sports centres, swimming pools and golf courses (ask at your local council Leisure Services department, Recreation department or Parks and Gardens department). Some restaurants and cafes have reduced rates for the unemployed, as do some hairdressers. Evening classes or courses at colleges are often free. There may be set times at all of these when you can use your UB40 so you will have to check before you go.

66

The UB40 can be used as a way of doing things cheaply.

99

What is available does depend on your area, so have a look around, check in the local newspapers, listen to the local radio station or ask at the Citizens Advice Bureau or Information Centre. There's no harm in asking at places which don't advertise reduced rates. You never know – they might agree, so it's useful to carry your UB40 with you at all times.

CONTINUING YOUR EDUCATION

You've had enough of school – or it's had enough of you – and you're thinking about continuing your education at college. You may be wanting to do a degree, to take your A levels away from school, or do a course that will qualify you for a particular type of work; you may already have four excellent A levels or a couple of low-level GCSEs. But whatever situation you are in, there will be a choice of different forms of further education available.

There are two main ways of continuing your education after you leave school – Further Education and Higher Education. Further Education (FE) Colleges are mainly for 16–19 year olds, although older people also attend. FE colleges cater for anybody – so whether or not you have any qualifications there will be a course to suit you. On the other hand, most Higher Education courses, such as those at universities, ask for A levels, or their equivalent.

Colleges run a variety of courses – full-time, part-time (day or evening) and day-release from work. Even if you left school some time ago you may still be able to benefit from a course, whether your aim is to improve your job prospects, increase your general level of education, or just to extend your leisure activities and social life.

Further education

If you think you are interested in going to a further education college your first and last port of call should be your local careers office. It doesn't matter if you missed seeing a careers officer at school. The careers office will have prospectuses and directories of courses, and there will be a careers officer to advise you on your choice of course. Your local library will also have details of courses.

You will find that there are several kinds of further education college. The most common is a College of Further Education, sometimes called a Technical College or College of Technology. They usually offer a wide range of courses, from general education such as English and maths, through to highly specialised vocational courses such as art and design, commerce and engineering.

Some areas have Tertiary Colleges, which combine sixth-form courses with other further education, and many parts of England and Wales have Sixth Form Colleges where often the emphasis is on academic courses, and only teach people aged between 16 and 19.

> **❝**
>
> **Many colleges have open days at which you can learn about them before applying.**
>
>

Although they teach some of the same courses as schools, all these colleges are very different from school and require a completely different approach to study. For a start, it is your decision whether you go to one, whereas your attendance at school up to the age of 16 is a legal requirement. Colleges usually offer a wider range of courses than schools, and tuition is in lectures of an hour or longer rather than in formal lessons. It is often down to you to ensure that work is handed in on time, and you will have to do a lot of work on your own, instead of finding that you are being pushed to do specific homework exercises. Colleges are usually situated on several sites instead of in one place, like most schools. In general, you will find at a college that you are treated more as an adult than at school, but correspondingly you have to take more responsibility for your own time.

If you're still debating about whether to leave school and the course you want can be done just as well by staying on, such as A levels or taking further GCSEs, weigh up the advantages and disadvantages of school and college carefully, remembering that these will be different for everybody. Many colleges have open days at which you can attend so as to learn about them while considering applying.

Which course?

There are three main types of course on offer at further education colleges – vocational, non-vocational and pre-vocational.

A vocational course is one which involves specialised training, usually for a particular career such as catering or building. A non-vocational course is more general, such as GCSEs or A levels. Sometimes the two may be combined, perhaps in a secretarial course. A pre-vocational course offers the opportunity to sample different occupational areas and could be appropriate if you have not decided what sort of employment you want.

There are also hundreds of part-time day and evening courses available, and some employers offer day-release to college for studies relevant to your job. If you are unemployed you may be able to do a part-time course of not longer than 21 hours a week and still claim benefit. (See the previous chapter.)

Which course you choose depends on a number of factors, always bearing in mind what you would eventually like to do. If you have a particular career in mind a vocational course that gives you a qualification for that kind of work may be right. If you are undecided, a more general education course may be better, giving you time to think about careers and assess your strengths and abilities. Your careers officer will be only too happy to help you.

If you are worried about whether the course will help you get a job, try to find out what jobs past students have found. The college should have records of this, but look behind the statistics – if all last year's students are working, did they actually get the sort of jobs they wanted? Check out what your qualifications will mean to an employer. The careers office can help with this.

Most colleges have careers advisers. They may have jobs on file – so once you're at college make and maintain contact with them. They may be able to let you know about jobs as they come in. They can also help you with your plans before you start a course.

GCSEs, Standard Grades and A Levels

Colleges frequently offer a broader range of GCSEs and A levels (Standard Grades and Highers in Scotland) than schools. Most colleges offer a special GCSE 'Mature' package, usually of about four subjects. However, think twice if you only have a few GCSEs below grade E but have found a college to take you on to do more. The success rate for such students is often very poor, which can be very disappointing. If you have done badly in academic subjects at school you may do far better on a practical course, which may even lead on to higher courses.

Most colleges will ask you to have at least four high-grade GCSEs of grade C or above before starting a two-year course of two or three A levels.

Certificate in Pre-Vocational Education (CPVE)

CPVE (also known as 17+) is a new qualification aimed at young people who would benefit from a course with a practical basis. No exam passes are required, and it may lead on to higher-level courses which normally require high-grade GCSEs or equivalent. CPVE involves being taught certain 'core' skills such as careers education, communication and problem-solving, and then vocational subjects, mainly business and administrative practices, technical services, production, distribution, and services to people (like catering or child care). At the end of CPVE you get a certificate and a profile of your progress which can be shown to employers. You can also combine the CPVE with one or two GCSEs. CPVE can be an excellent opportunity for you if traditional school study methods did not suit you. It lasts for a year.

There is no CPVE in Scotland, but a National Certificate instead, which is a part of the 16–18 Government Action Plan. Like CPVE it is a flexible system, with a bias towards vocational studies. It can be taken up on a full-time basis, or part-time in conjunction with a YTS or other employment. Full time, the courses last a year, but can be spread over two or three years when done on day release.

Vocational Courses

Vocational courses taught at Further Education colleges are set up by various organisations that determine the curricula and the awarding of qualifications.

The City and Guilds of London Institute runs a wide range of technical courses, many of which do not require exam passes. Available courses vary from hairdressing to building, from musical instrument technology to fashion. Many operate as day-release courses from jobs, and are generally well-recognised by employers. Full-time courses are also available. For more information on the courses and colleges where they are taught write to City and Guilds of London Institute, 76 Portland Place, London W1N 4AA.

The Royal Society for the Encouragement of Arts, Manufacture and Commerce (RSA) runs vocational courses in business studies and office skills as well as in English, maths, and English as a foreign language. Write to The Royal Society of Arts Examination Board, John Adam Street, London WC2N 6EZ.

The Business and Technician Education Council (BTEC) runs vocational courses for people with GCSEs and A levels. In Scotland SCOTVEC runs similar courses. It is likely that you will be able to progress from CPVE to BTEC if you leave school without any qualifications. BTEC courses include business and finance, engineering, art and design. They provide nationally recognised training for a number of careers.

For BTEC technical courses, the minimum entry requirement is usually good grade GCSEs. However, you might get in without any formal entry requirements since there is an entrance test for many courses.

On the business side, there are two main levels of BTEC. You usually need four high-grade GCSEs for the BTEC National Certificate or Diploma, which lasts two years and can also be done on a day-release basis from a job. For the BTEC Higher National Certificate, A levels or a BTEC National qualification are required. For more information write to BTEC Information Office, Central House, Upper Woburn Place, London WC1 0HH, or SCOTVEC (Scottish Vocational Education Council), 22 Great King Street, Edinburgh EH3 6QH.

Some colleges run specialised foundation courses, for example in art and design or accountancy, which usually require GCSEs and often lead to further courses.

There are now a number of college courses financed by the Youth Training Scheme (Youth Training Programme in Northern Ireland). These are often a good alternative to an ordinary college course with the added benefit of the YTS allowance (currently £29.50 pw) and a period of work experience. Some people even get jobs through their work experience. At present you have to be 16 or 17 to be eligible for YTS. Ask at a Jobcentre or Careers Office, and see the previous chapter.

It is worth noting that many colleges are flexible regarding their entry requirements, treating each case on its own merits. For many courses, relevant experience or particular abilities may be more important. For example, for artistic courses such as photography or art more weight will be attached to the portfolio of your work than your exam passes. So if your exam qualifications are poor it is still worth writing to the college to enquire about a course you want to do.

Special Needs

If you are disabled, or speak very little English, it may be that your local college runs a special course to meet your needs. There are sometimes lots of courses available if you have a disability or are linguistically disadvantaged. Exam passes are not always required.

Applications

To apply to any Further Education college, first read its prospectus, which you can obtain by telephoning or writing to the college (address from the careers office). Compare courses and entry requirements.

Then write or telephone for an application form. Complete it in pencil first – get it checked – then fill it in neatly in ink. Tell the college all about yourself – your interests, hobbies and favourite school subjects. Apply early – before Christmas for popular courses, and try to arrange a visit to the college. Talk to the other students and find out what they think of it.

You may wait some time before being called for an interview, so don't worry if you do not hear right away. At the interview you must prove your interest and determination to work hard to the college staff. For certain courses you may be given an aptitude test.

After the interview the college will write to you to let you know whether you have been successful. It may offer you a place on the condition that you reach a certain standard in your examinations.

Grants

Until you are 19 course fees are usually paid by your local education authority, although you should always check this before starting a course. Maintenance grants for further education courses are usually discretionary, which means that it is up to your local authority to decide whether or not you get one. Generally if an award is made it is only very small, and is assessed on the basis of your parents' income. However, if you are doing a full-time course, your parents or guardians should be able to claim child benefit for you until you are 19.

Write to your Local Education Authority Awards Section for more information (Education and Library Board in Northern Ireland).

If you do have money worries whilst at college there is usually a counsellor or Student Services Officer to help. They can help with other problems as well.

Higher education

A degree may no longer be the only passport to a high-flying job, but higher education qualifications are still very popular with employers, and with heavy competition for the number of places available you need to be especially well-informed before applying.

Higher education does not begin and end with a degree; it also covers studying for a diploma or some professional qualification. For nearly all the courses offered you need to have A levels (Highers in Scotland), although for some college diplomas good GCSEs are sufficient. Degree courses last three or four years, and involve going either to a university, a polytechnic, or a College or Institute of Higher Education. Polytechnics and Colleges and Institutes of Higher Education also offer diplomas of Higher Education, which are two-year courses. They are below degree level, but after taking the diploma you may be able to transfer to the third year of a degree course. Colleges of Further and Higher Education offer another qualification just below degree level, the BTEC Higher National Certificate or Diploma, with a comparable diploma awarded in Scotland by SCOTVEC.

Not all these courses are full-time; many are offered on a part-time basis, whether degrees or diplomas. Some courses, particularly in technical subjects, include a period spent working in industry, and are known as 'sandwich' courses.

Applications

Handbooks on higher education can seem awfully dull, but if you do read them they will eventually guide you to courses which may suit you. The college prospectuses are also important reading; many colleges issue in addition an 'alternative prospectus', usually written by students, which may give a more honest view of the college! Try to visit the college if you can before accepting a place – if you are going to spend two or three years there you need to get a 'feel' of the place to see if you think you will be happy.

A useful introductory booklet is *Higher Education – Finding Your Way* by David Dixon, HMSO, and for degrees *Degree Course Offers* by Brian Heep, published by Careers Consultants and *Degree Course Guides* and *Which Degree*, published by CRAC.

All applications for first degree courses at universities are dealt with by the Universities Central Council on Admissions (UCCA). You complete only one form (an UCCA form) which allows you to give an order preference for a maximum of five universities. This is obtained from your school or college, or direct from UCCA, PO Box 28, Cheltenham, Gloucestershire GL50 1HY.

The closing date for submitting your application is mid-October for Oxford and Cambridge and mid-December for all others (the actual date varies). There is a small application fee. Essential reading is the *Compendium of University Entry Requirements, The Sunday Times Good University Guide* and *The Student Book* (published annually).

The Polytechnics Central Admission System (PCAS) now deals with all applications for degree and DipHE courses in polytechnics (but not initial teacher training or art and design which have their own systems). Like UCCA there is one form – but with four choices and no order of preference. PCAS then send your form to the polytechnics of your choice. The closing date is mid-December and there is a small fee. There are no polytechnics in

"Your results aren't up to much but I'll admit your portfolio is impressive."

Scotland, and only one in Northern Ireland, which is not part of the PCAS system. You should apply directly to it.

All non-university art and design degree applications are administered by the Art and Design Admissions Registry, 24 Widemarsh Street, Hereford HR4 8EP. You normally need to have completed a foundation course in art and design before getting into one of these – ask at the careers office for details.

All applications for teacher training are dealt with centrally by The Central Register and Clearing House, 3 Crawford Place, London W1H 2BN. You list three colleges in order of preference on the application form.

For most other types of course, applications are made directly to the college concerned. However, sometimes the Central Register and Clearing House deals with degree applications – details will be given in the prospectus of the college concerned. It is worth noting that some colleges of higher education offer degrees that are validated by a university. The entry requirements are usually lower than other university degrees.

Applications for certain specialist courses including physio-therapy and social work are administered through their own clearing houses. Ask at the careers office for more information.

If you want to apply for a higher education course after you have left school, you will find that many higher education establishments look favourably upon 'mature applicants' (usually people over the age of 21, although this can vary), and entrance requirements may be lower. The admissions procedure for UCCA and PCAS is still the same; write to them direct.

Many further education colleges run 'Access to Higher Education' courses for people without the traditional entry requirements.

If you can't commit yourself to full-time study, there are numerous part-time courses on offer. The Open University (OU) has proved extremely popular. It is open to anyone over 18 living in the UK, and teaches both degree and non-degree short courses. Teaching is by a mixture of correspondence and TV and radio programmes, but you are also linked to a personal tutor.

> **66**
> **If you can't commit yourself to full-time study, there are numerous part-time courses on offer.**
> **99**

You do not have to have GCSEs or A levels, but the work is hard. OU courses have to be paid for, but some of the fees may be covered by your local authority. The Open University's address is PO Box 76, Milton Keynes MK7 6AN.

Grants and loans

The government is committed ultimately to phasing out the system of grants which provides financial support for higher-education students. Grants themselves will remain in existence for several years to come, but according to plans current at the time of writing, they are to be frozen at their 1989 levels. In order to keep up with inflation students are to be invited to get 'top-up' loans, which will eventually have to be paid back. Year by year, as the value of money declines, grants will become worth less and less and the 'top-up' loans will represent a larger proportion of student incomes.

The grant element is something you are entitled to by law from your local authority, providing certain conditions are met. First, they are only available for 'designated courses' which are: university or CNAA first degree, Diploma in Higher Education, BTEC Higher National Diploma, initial and post-graduate teacher training, university certificate or diploma of at least three years' duration, and other qualifications comparable to a first degree.

In addition, you must have been resident in the UK for the three years before the academic year in which your course begins, and you must not have already attended a course of advanced further education of more than two years' duration. If you do not qualify for a mandatory award, a discretionary grant may be paid to you.

Apply for the grant in plenty of time, any time from March onwards of the year you are going to college. If you qualify for a grant, your fees (ie the costs of teaching you) will be paid and you will also get a contribution to your living expenses. The size of the grant is assessed according to your own and your parents' income. In 1989–90 – and thus the levels at which grants are likely to be fixed – if you were at a college and living in a hall of residence, a flat or lodgings, the maximum rates were £2650 in London and £2155 elsewhere. If you lived at your parents' home the maximum was £1710, which was also sometimes the maximum if you could live at home but chose not to.

However, depending on your parents' income, you will not usually get these full amounts, but only a part. Your parents are expected to make up the sum. You do get a full grant, though, if you are 25 before the start of the course, or if you have been self-supporting for three years before the start of the course.

A useful free booklet, 'Grants to Students: a brief guide', is obtainable from The Department of Education and Science, Publications Despatch Centre, Honeypot Lane, Canons Park, Stanmore, Middlesex HA7 1AZ.

In Northern Ireland write for a leaflet entitled 'Grants to Students', to The Department of Education, Rathgael House, Balloo Road, Bangor, County Down BT19 2PR.

In Scotland write for the leaflet called 'Guide to Students' Allowances' from The Scottish Education Department, New St Andrew's House, St James Centre, Edinburgh EH1 3SY.

Sponsorships

Each year a number of firms and professional organisations sponsor promising students on higher education courses. An award is normally payable in addition to the student grant. Many sponsorships are for 'sandwich courses', and you are expected to work for the firm during your period in industry (although you are paid!). You may be expected to spend a period of time, say two years, with the firm once you have graduated.

Part-time study

Whether you're working, unemployed or a full-time student, you may be interested in one or more of the thousands of part-time courses available throughout the country. These cover GCSE and A levels, professional qualifications and a vast range of subjects which may be broadly defined as 'leisure'. If you are unemployed you might be able to do a 21-hour course and still claim benefit (see p. 59).

Local colleges will tell you about their part-time courses. Adult Education Institutes and the Workers' Educational Association also run part-time courses which include almost anything from jazz singing to flower arranging, from intermediate French to car maintenance. You usually have to attend one evening a week, and there is a small charge for the course. While you can do GCSEs on specific courses, most are only run for interest, so there's no need to worry if you've had your fill of exams! Local libraries have details of courses available, while in London you can buy *Floodlight*, which lists all the evening classes in the London area.

If you are working full-time you may be able to attend college on a day-release basis, perhaps one day a week. This may lead to a professional qualification. Ask your employer – but he or she may be more likely to send you if you have shown your interest by giving up an evening or two to attend an appropriate evening class. Your local college, library or careers office will have details of courses.

What to expect from your new life

Once you get to college or university you will find that it is not like a continuation of school. You'll be more your own boss. Ultimately though, what you can expect from going to college will depend on what level you are studying at.

If you go into higher education you'll discover a ready made social life. You'll be coping for yourself, and enjoying the independence once you start to make a go of it. You will also find that no-one chases you for essays or practical work – you may be given written work deadlines at the beginning of the year or term, but it's up to you to meet them. How you organise your work time is largely your own concern – though if you don't do any work you are likely to be thrown out!

> **66**
>
> **How you organise your work time is largely your concern.**
>
> **99**

It's difficult to generalise about the way your workload will be presented to you, however. The college prospectus will outline how the teaching of your particular courses is structured and this will be explained to you in detail during your first week. A typical pattern consists of non-compulsory lectures, and tutorial groups of a small number of students where essays are set and discussed. You may be expected to produce one or more essays a week plus practical work where relevant, and your marks may

75

be used as part of a continuous assessment which contributes towards your final degree or diploma. On the other hand the teaching may well be more formal, especially where colleges are having to economise.

Going into further education depends on the attitude of the individual college authorities. Some college principals still think of themselves as in charge of older school kids. Also further education colleges are becoming the alternative to the dole for lots of people, so it is all the more important on both counts to find out about the place before you apply.

If you go to a further education college you are also likely still to be living at home, whereas most students in higher education have chosen somewhere away from home.

Social life

The social centre of college life is the student union. In big colleges it can run bars, discos, shops, welfare advice centres and even laundrettes. It will run clubs and societies catering for every sporting, social and cultural interest. In smaller colleges its activities may be limited to selling college sweatshirts and running the once-a-term gig. Further education colleges often have problems getting a bar licence, due to having students under the age of 18.

You may find that the higher education college up the road will allow local further education students to use some of its facilities on production of the National Union of Students (NUS) card. 98 per cent of colleges in Britain are members of NUS, and today more than half of NUS members are under 18, so whatever level you're studying at make sure you get your membership card from your student union office. Your membership is automatic, and any subscription is deducted at source from your grant.

As well as social facilities, student unions represent your interests while you are at college. That can range from selling you cheap beer and food to representing you at an appeal against an academic decision. In universities and polytechnics student unions are recognised as a vital part of the institution, though sometimes in further education colleges they are seen as an irritation by principals who think they know what's best for you.

Getting involved in student politics through the student union is a good introduction to the world of politics in general (see 'Politics' chapter). College careers advisers agree that today potential employers look as much at 'personal skills' (such as the ability to organise or work in a team) as academic ones, and a student union is the natural place to acquire them. Whether it be running the debating society, doing community work, writing for the college paper, or being elected union president, you can get involved in things that will make your time at college more enjoyable and worthwhile. A recent president of NUS started off collecting signatures against a rule which banned girlfriends from students' bedrooms, so whatever you decide to do – whether just making use of the canteen, bar or sports facilities, or getting more actively involved – you never know where you may end up!

However, your life won't be entirely student union based. Most colleges and universities have subsidised arts centres where you can see films, plays, concerts (popular *and* classical) and ballets, performed either by local groups or touring companies; they also put on art and photography exhibitions and often have coffee shops, bars or restaurants which give you an alternative meeting place. Arts centres are usually open to the general public and charge accordingly, but you'll almost certainly get price concessions as a student. A well-run arts centre can be a boon if you're at a campus-based university which is some distance from a large town.

Universities and polytechnics often have access to excellent sports facilities (their own or a nearby institution's) and FE colleges sometimes offer sports facilities as well. Popular sports like swimming, tennis, squash, basketball, gymnastics and the usual team sports can be enjoyed all year round and some have access to water sports as well. Sports centres are usually open to college staff as well, but not always to the general public.

All colleges have their own libraries; most universities also have a large centralised library which services the colleges and lends in its own right. You will be given all the details of the library system at your particular college within a few days of arriving for your first term.

Most large colleges and universities have representatives of or centres for the main religions. Even if you don't belong to a religion you'll be welcome to visit and if you've got any problems it can be helpful to talk to a minister or priest that you find sympathetic. There will also be a student health centre offering the full range of health care and saving you the bother of finding a temporary GP or dentist if you're away from home. The health centre will probably provide contraception and counselling services as well.

And don't forget that universities and colleges have their own careers services, admittedly some better than others! Many departments have their own links with industry and the professions and some enterprising universities and polytechnics have actually pooled their resources with industrial concerns in so-called 'science parks' where university-based research is developed commercially.

All these general facilities and any others offered by your college or university will be detailed in the prospectus. It's a good idea to read it thoroughly so you can have some idea of what's laid on before you go.

Unless you're doing a full-time vocational course at FE college, which tends to fill up your day pretty effectively, you'll probably find you've got a lot more free time than you're used to. If you're away from home as well you may find that you cannot afford to return very often at weekends even if you want to. If you are lonely and are finding it hard to mix, don't mope alone. The student union exists to help with personal and practical problems. Anything to do with your life inside or outside college that's worrying you can be shared with experienced and sympathetic people who've often been through the same problems themselves, so go and see them. Alternatively, one of the college chaplains, a doctor or counsellor at the health centre, your warden of hall or your personal tutor are all there to help; go to them for confidential advice.

Where to live

For many young people part of the process of choosing where to study is deciding whether or not to leave home. For further education students the choice is limited by the fact that discretionary grants are only paid to those attending the local further education college. Matters are further confused by the tangle of regulations over eligibility for housing and other benefits. But for a higher education student, going to college can represent a cushioned break with the family home.

The idea of gaining your independence as being part of the learning process is now generally accepted in higher education circles.

Of course some people will actually prefer to go to a local college, so as to remain at home in an area or circle of friends they've grown up in. If staying at home is your choice, fair enough. However, if it seems too much like an extension of school life, or you just fancy moving on from home, then going to college can provide a golden opportunity.

Although under no legal obligation to do so, most higher education colleges accept their responsibility to provide accommodation for at least a proportion of their students. The idea of leaving home and gaining your independence as being part of the learning process is now generally accepted in higher education circles, if not by government education ministers.

Universities are better provided with halls of residence than other colleges, though even they have problems housing all their students. In general, first year, disabled and overseas students get top priority, with students facing final exams being considered if there's room to spare. About 180,000 (35 per cent) of higher education students live 'in hall'. These can vary from the ivy-covered buildings of Oxford and Cambridge, to the breezeblock towers of the more modern colleges. Some will be on campus near teaching and social facilities, while others may be a distance away, possibly with their own bar and facilities. Some are self-catering, with kitchen facilities for up to a dozen students, while others offer full board with meals served or available in self-service cafeterias.

Most halls have two things in common – high rents and a number of regulations. Halls with full board currently cost about £55 a week in London, and £45 per week elsewhere. Self-catering is cheaper, with current prices around £25 per week in London, and just over £19 per week elsewhere.

Regulations and restrictions will vary from place to place, often depending on if the hall is mixed or single-sex. Some mixed halls are very easy-going, while the more traditional ones can be run like boarding schools or army barracks, with no visitors allowed after certain hours. But whatever the circumstances, halls do mean you meet other new students from the moment you arrive, so loneliness isn't a problem.

If you don't manage to secure a place in a hall straight away, make sure you get your name on the college Accommodation Officer's waiting list. Vacancies often occur as students drop out after a few weeks of term, or don't turn up in the first place.

Some colleges operate Head Tenancy schemes, where they lease property direct from private landlords and then sub-let the accommodation to their students. Again, your college accommodation office will advise you of these.

You may decide against college accommodation from the start – some people don't fancy the idea of sharing kitchen and bathroom facilities with up to a dozen others – and look elsewhere. Most students seeking an alternative have to rely on renting from a private landlord.

About 94 per cent of students outside of halls of residence are in this situation, so there can be a great deal of competition for private rented housing, especially in urban areas where a high proportion of local housing is owned by the council and not generally available to students. So, rents can often be quite high. The average rent (per student) in the private sector for 1984–85 was between £17 and £25 per week. It is interesting to note that between 35 and 40 per cent of a student's income is spent on rent – that's more than even the poorest families in Britain.

Apart from private flats, bedsits and houses, you may want to consider digs or lodgings. This may conjur up pictures of ageing landladies in curlers, but you are more likely to find yourself lodging with a young family or single parent. You will be expected to turn up for meals on time, and rents may be higher than the average for the private sector, but given the right household regulations should be minimal.

In recent years, as student numbers have risen, colleges have found it increasingly difficult to house all their students at the start of the academic year. The trick is to secure some sort of accommodation, through the college accommodation office, as soon as you can. If you are late in signing up for your course, and arrive at college without anywhere to stay, go and see the Accommodation Officer right away. He or she usually has lists of local accommodation, and will help if possible. At a pinch your student union may be able to arrange short-term emergency accommodation, though this is likely to be a bit rough. Your best bet is to leave nothing to chance, and get yourself fixed up with somewhere before you leave home.

Budgeting

Since rent and living expenses (food, heat, light, travel) are going to be your biggest financial outlay, how you budget will depend very much on where you are living. If you have a place in hall, you are normally expected to pay your rent for the term in advance, and if you're looking to move into private rented accommodation, remember that most landlords will require a fair-sized deposit.

For many people, getting a grant cheque will mean opening a bank account for the first time, and many banks offer an advisory service to students, as well as some attractive deals (see p. 90). But never forget that the banks are all competing for a slice of the student market, and their seeming generosity has limits. Most are now offering cheque books and guaranteed overdrafts, so the temptation to overspend is worse than ever.

The big danger is getting too deep into overdraft. Going overdrawn at the end of term bites into next term's grant before you've even picked up the cheque, and this can have a 'knock-on' effect. In order to get by on a grant you have to organise your money – before you spend it. You should be able to work out a budget for the term ahead, knowing how much you are going to need for rent and the rest.

> **Going overdrawn at the end of term bites into next term's grant before you've even picked up the cheque.**

As far as books, stationery and other essentials are concerned, find out about student discount deals that exist with local shops – your student union will have details. Some student unions even run their own shops and mini-supermarkets, with lower prices than elsewhere. At the start of the year you'll find students from the previous year selling their textbooks off cheap, often through the union shop.

When you are budgeting, don't overlook the cost of seeing yourself through the Christmas and Easter breaks. Your grant is supposed to cover the cost of these, but it rarely does, and many students either get a temporary job or have to rely on their parents.

Students and the DSS

At the time of writing students over the age of 16 are entitled to claim certain DSS benefits.

Currently, if you are in higher education your grant is expected to cover you for the short vacations, but you are entitled to claim unemployment benefit during the long summer holiday providing that you have made enough National Insurance contributions (see p. 18) and are available and willing to work. If you are in (non-advanced) further education, and are between the ages of 16 and 19, you are usually excluded from claiming during both term and holiday time.

Further education students who pay rent however may be eligible for housing benefit (see p. 167), as may higher education students. Many in higher education successfully claim housing benefit during the summer vacation, and depending on the level of rent paid can top up their grants during the rest of the year providing they are not renting direct from the college or university. Since higher education students are treated as having no income during the summer break (unless they find a job) they are currently entitled to claim income support, and with this entitlement comes certificated housing benefit covering 80 per cent of rent, but this is being abolished with the introduction of student loans.

Students who face financial hardships during a vacation may be able to get a vacation hardship allowance from their council. If you think you might qualify, apply to your local education authority.

The government has threatened to abolish student rights to social security altogether, which until recently were far more extensive. Welfare benefits in the long vacation must be regarded as being in jeopardy.

Transferring courses

Many students find during the early part of their studies that for one reason or another they are dissatisfied with their choice of course. Before doing anything final, you should be clear in your own mind exactly what you are unhappy with. Difficulty in settling into college life may not be solved by simply moving to another college. Likewise, a personality clash with a certain tutor may not in the long run be enough reason for throwing away your plans for the future.

Once you have examined your motives and decided that a change – either to another course or to another college – is best, there are people you can talk to, such as college welfare staff or the student union. However, the ultimate decision is in the hands of the academics, and you must get the agreement of the staff running your course or department.

Then there's the money angle to think about. If you are self-financing, then you can work out these considerations for yourself. If you're a further education student on a discretionary grant you'll need to consult your local education authority and check that they will continue to provide finance after your change.

For students in higher education on mandatory grants there are two conditions that must be satisfied for payment to continue. Firstly, you must get the OK from the academics, from your current college if you are simply changing course, or from both institutions if you are transferring to another college. Secondly, you must transfer within fourteen months of the start of your course, or, if later, then the date you finish the new course must be no later than the date you would have finished the original course. If you don't satisfy these conditions you will only be eligible for a discretionary award.

MONEY MATTERS

Leaving school means assuming responsibility for your own finances, learning how money works and how to make the most of it. While some of the contents of this chapter may not apply to you at the moment, there will come a time when you need to know about insurance, tax and savings, and it may be sooner than you think.

Especially if your means are slender, the art of managing your money is a technique you should acquire now, if you are not to fall into debt – all too easy to do, even if you are still living at home. The clue to living within your income is successful budgeting.

Budgeting

You are bound to know one. Everybody does. I am talking about that individual who is always in the money. His parents are not rich. And, as far as you can tell, he would never steal. Or, her Saturday jobs were not any more lucrative than yours and her granny was not always slipping her a tenner. And though occasionally they helped old ladies across the street, none has yet made them her heir. Nevertheless they always have the cash to buy a record, the entrance for the disco and their bus fare home. Their secret is budgeting: they make the best of what they have and eke out limited funds by careful planning.

This is the skill you too must acquire if you are to keep out of debt, but still be well-fed and able to take the occasional pleasure.

Your first task is to add together your income from all sources (salary, grant, cash from covenant and holiday jobs, or dole and other benefits). Then draw up a schedule of your out-goings, using the following checklist as guidance:

- Rent, Hall of Residence fees or mortgage repayments
- Telephone
- Gas
- Electricity
- Daily travel costs
- Insurance premiums
- Food
- Toiletries (shampoo, razors, make-up)
- Hair cuts
- Medicines
- Presents
- Clothes
- Books and magazines
- Records and tapes
- TV rental, cinema
- Drinks and cigarettes
- Holidays

If you can't manage to compile a list of your spending, take a notebook around with you for a month and write down religiously everything you spend. Your friends may think you're mad, but they may equally presume you are jotting down ideas for some great novel. Either way, if the total of your expenditure exceeds that of your income then you either continue to live on an expanding overdraft or attempt to cut down.

Look down the list – where can you slash your spending? If you have regular travel commitments to and from work, buy a season ticket or better still a bike. If it's only a couple of miles – walk. And how about reading magazines in the hairdresser's rather than buying them, and scanning the papers in the reference library? Give up cigarettes and save your life as well as your money. Food is one of the areas where the most substantial savings can be made: you do not need steak!

Try not to patronise late-night corner shops except in dire emergencies: their prices are invariably higher. Buy in street markets and the big cut-price supermarkets. Fresh vegetables and fruit are cheaper in the long run than convenience foods. When you buy high-margin items like biscuits, you are paying for a lot of useless packaging.

You may be reading this book still filled with the glee that seizes everyone when they set aside school uniform forever. Certainly you will need new clothes, but don't run amok – more budgets have been bust in clothes stores than anywhere else. Think very carefully whether the items you like will be hard-wearing, or will need expensive dry cleaning as opposed to just washing.

Besides finding ways and means to curtail your spending, explore the possibilities of boosting your income. Are you claiming all the benefits you're entitled to? (Read 'Which Benefit', available from the DSS.)

Anyone with serious problems about making ends meet, or who finds themselves in debt to various lenders (credit card companies, banks, etc.) should ask for help from the Citizens Advice Bureau – their counselling comes free.

Where to keep your money

However much you may like the idea, it's hardly practical any more to keep your money in an old sock or under the mattress – and it's asking for trouble to carry it around with you in rolls of used fivers. Once you've got a regular income you need to keep it somewhere safe but accessible. The main choices are banks, building societies and the Post Office. Although some of the big building societies are beginning to offer services like banks, their main concern is still to attract savings and lend mortgages. The Post Office administers a banking service, as well as the Savings Bank which you may already have been using or used as a child.

Banks and banking

Like it or not, you will find yourself having to deal with the banking system, and unless you're under 18 and unemployed, you'll need to open some kind of bank account.

ACCOUNT NO. 7364920011;
SAVINGS ACCOUNT 5778; BARCLAYCARD
0023466923; PIN NO 813; ACCESS
37609511265; CHEQUE
CODE 88-11-63;
CREDIT 36p.

Though you might prefer to conduct all your financial transactions in cash, almost everyone else you come across who has anything to do with money will be using cheques or some other form of bank transaction. Most employers have, for example, now abandoned the traditional buff wage packet stuffed with comforting notes and coins. Instead you will either receive a cheque, accompanied by a computer-printed or hand-written slip, detailing the amount of your net pay, or a computer-printed slip detailing what has been transferred by the company straight into a bank or similar account. Equally, students cannot expect to be handed their grants in used fivers. Instead the local authority writes the undergraduate a cheque.

Even the DSS is getting into the act. Until recently, all social security recipients were to be seen queueing at post offices to cash their fortnightly Giro cheques. But, following some gentle persuasion, some are now visiting their banks to collect the money which is paid by the Department directly into their accounts.

The majority of these are, however, older people who have held bank accounts for years. They like the new system because for them it is both convenient and confidential. But if you are a young school-leaver on YTS you may not want to bother with a bank until your income has improved. For a start, in spite of the advertising you may find the banks less than eager to take you on. And secondly, even if you do succeed in becoming a customer, having a cheque book is a great temptation to overspend.

Choosing a bank

When you do decide to open an account, take some time choosing between the different banks. Do not stroll into the first branch you spy or opt automatically for the bank that has always enjoyed your parents' custom or that was the guardian of your savings account when you were young. The bank that gave you that sweet piggy bank when you were seven may not be the bank that offers you the best deal at seventeen. Any cash held in a junior account with one bank can easily be transferred into any new account you open. Indeed, with the widening of services offered by building societies you might prefer not to use a traditional bank at all.

> **The bank that gave you that sweet piggy bank when you were seven may not be the bank that offers you the best deal at seventeen.**

Begin the quest for a bank to suit you in your high street. Walk into every branch and pick up the leaflet that details what the Listening or Action Bank has on offer for the young. Bear in mind that there are other players on the British banking scene than the four big names – Barclays, Lloyds, the Midland and the National Westminster. The smaller banks such as the Co-op, the National Girobank (originally owned by the Post Office and still based in the nation's 26,000 post offices), the Trustee Savings Bank, the Bank of Scotland and the Yorkshire Bank also have their advantages. None of the banks now extract bank charges from you so long as you keep your account in credit for the *whole* of one accounting period – usually three months. Bank charges are fees you have to pay the bank for the service they offer. You pay each time you write a cheque or have a standing order paid, as each of these transactions involves the bank in some work. Charges are usually debited from your account directly by the bank, so the first you know about them may often be when you get your monthly or quarterly statement. This can be a blow when you have been budgeting carefully to your last penny – only to find you are paying charges because of being overdrawn once. Make sure you find out exactly what the charges are before you open an account. Charges are not standardised between the banks – for instance the charge for an 'automated transaction' (ie getting cash from a hole-in-the-wall machine) can vary between about 20p and 30p.

Though they may not prove to be so kindly in the future, the banks are all eagerness to take you on while you are young. If you're about to enter employment for the first time you can expect special treatment – a package that includes a cheque book, a cheque guarantee card (so-called because it guarantees to other people that your cheques up to the value of £50 will be paid by the bank, however little money you may have in the account), and also a cash card which enables you to withdraw money from the bank's system of 'automated tellers' – hole-in-the-wall cash machines. Often the cash card and the guarantee card are one and the same piece of plastic.

Students are also targets for the banks' marketing attentions, and are wooed with such blandishments as half-price coach travel and cheap overdrafts. The banks believe that today's impecunious undergraduate may be tomorrow's highly paid executive, willing to pay for the bank's various expensive additional services.

There are other practical factors in choosing a bank. Students should, for instance, discover whether there is a branch on or near the campus of their college and everyone should establish how accessible their funds will be from John O' Groats to Lands End. Will there be a 'hole-in-the-wall' cash machine wherever you go in Britain? Will you be able to use the machines of another bank? (For instance the machines operated by the Midland are open to NatWest customers, and vice versa.) What kind of deal does the bank offer in the future? When your student days are over will the bank help tide you over with a cheap loan until you find a job?

Once you have found your bank, simply call in and ask to open a current account. You will be required to sign a form or two, provide a few personal details and proof of your identity. To set up the account, you need just £1.

Overdrafts

Anyone who 'overdraws' – in other words spends more money than he or she has in the bank – will incur high charges, because the bank is actually lending you the money that you have overspent. However, if as a student you go to your bank manager for a personal loan of £100–£200, you may be lent the money at a cheaper rate, and some banks have schemes where regular earners can regularly overdraw up to a predetermined limit at not too heinous rates of interest.

In most cases, the interest payable is set at 'base rate plus one per cent', which is in fact considerably cheaper than the rate paid by other personal customers. ('Base rate' or minimum lending rate is the rate of interest fixed by the Treasury and the Bank of England as a minimum interest rate for loans. Most other rates of bank interest to the ordinary customer are higher than base rate.)

It is wise not to get on the wrong side of the manager for the heinous crime of an unauthorised overdraft. He may stop payment of your cheques, 'bouncing' them, which means sending them back to the payees, who will immediately bounce them back to you. This is an embarrassing experience even if you have the hide of a rhino, quite apart from the expense of an unauthorised overdraft.

Cheques

Before you write out your first cheque, take a look at the anatomy of a cheque opposite. There is more to the process than developing a stylish signature. Write clearly, using a pen or biro, never a pencil. Do not leave gaps between words since this allows the unscrupulous to add to or change them. Always fill in the cheque stub as well so that you can check your statement when it comes (see below).

Nowadays shops usually want your cheque to be supported by a cheque guarantee card, so have it with you if you're intending to pay by cheque. The shop assistant will ask to see your card, will compare the signature on card and cheque and write the number on the back of the cheque.

Do not keep your cheque book and card together – doing so makes fraud simple for the thief.

If you want to withdraw money from your account go to a branch of your bank and write 'Cash' on the 'Pay' line of your cheque. At the branch where your account is lodged, you can withdraw as much cash as you like, but at any other branch you must produce your card and keep within the £50 limit. You can also withdraw cash from other banks but some will make a charge for the service.

Paying-in slips

If you want to pay money into your account either by cheque or in cash you fill in a paying-in slip. Most banks interleave some of these in your cheque book, stamped with your account number and bank details like a cheque. If you have a lot of deposits (for instance, if you're self-employed or paid by cheque or cash rather than directly into your account) you can ask for a

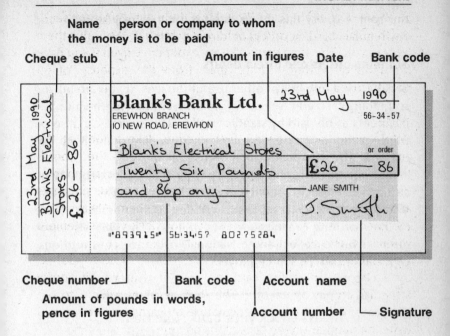

Name — person or company to whom the money is to be paid

Cheque stub

Amount in figures

Date

Bank code

Blank's Bank Ltd.
EREWHON BRANCH
IO NEW ROAD, EREWHON

23rd May 1990

56-34-57

Blank's Electrical Stores

or order

Twenty Six Pounds
and 86p only —

£26 — 86

JANE SMITH

J. Smith

"893915" 56·34·57 80275284

Cheque number
Amount of pounds in words, pence in figures

Bank code

Account name
Account number

Signature

Paying-In Book, which contains a number of slips. Fill in the counterfoils of your paying-in slips just as you would a cheque; the bank teller will stamp them as a receipt. When your statement comes you can check whether the right amount of money has been paid into your account. You can usually pay in to any bank and they will pass your deposit on to your own bank branch.

Statements

Each cheque you write is 'debited' (or withdrawn) from your account, while any money you pay in will be 'credited'. These transactions will appear on a quarterly statement of your account that the bank will send you. (You can ask for it to be sent monthly but you should check if this will incur higher charges.) It is worthwhile acquiring the habit of checking this statement – computers are not infallible. You will also be able to see what charges are being taken direct from your account by the bank – query this if you don't think they're justified – and any regular standing orders or 'direct debits'.

Standing orders and direct debits

Banks have a number of other useful services. If you are buying something on credit (see p. 104) you can arrange for the monthly payments to be paid by standing order. This system can also be used for rent or mortgage payments (providing definitive proof of payment), rates or any other regular bills.

Another form of automatic bill paying is by direct debit. Many companies offer this service, especially if it involves an annual sum such as for a magazine subscription or membership of one of the motoring organisations like the AA. The DSS also uses direct debit to collect some National Insurance contributions, especially from the self-employed.

> **Always check your bank statement carefully if you have a direct debit arrangement.**

It works by the company's bank arranging for the money to be removed directly from your account to theirs. If you're offered a direct debit arrangement read the agreement carefully before you sign it. The company has the right to vary the amount they take although they must notify you of how much this is. This may be all right for the DSS which has to make periodic adjustments to things like NI contributions, but you may not like to give a commercial company this freedom. Always check your bank statement carefully if you have a direct debit arrangement to make sure the payments are being made correctly.

Some banks run budget accounts which help to get you over the problem of large quarterly bills. More information on how to run a bank account will be contained in the stack of leaflets you will be given when you open the account. Do not throw these straight into the bin but read them first – they also include other useful advice on such subjects as balancing your budget.

Saving

Saving may not be your first imperative at present but since the habit or the need may creep up on you it is useful to know something about it.

Bank deposit accounts

Millions of people choose to save with their banks, opening 'seven day' deposit accounts which pay a rate of interest which isn't particularly good. (Generally speaking, the banks reserve their best rates for larger investors.)

Building Societies

You will probably get a better deal at a building society, and if you have even £5 a month to spare you should consider leaving it in the care of one of Britain's 180-odd societies.

Make a friend of your building society manager now and he will look favourably on you when you want to buy your own home. Such an idea may be unimaginable at the moment, but rented accommodation costs a great deal and is in short supply so it is easy to find yourself paying out more to a landlord than you would for a mortgage (see p. 154).

Building societies offer several different types of savings account, depending on how much money you have. If you can only put by a small amount on a regular basis an ordinary account is probably all you need. It pays interest on the money you have deposited all the time and you can withdraw cash at any time the office is open without having to give notice. If you manage to save a reasonable amount – or maybe you come by a nest egg in the form of a legacy perhaps – or if you intend to save on a long-term basis, you will find most societies offer special accounts which offer a much higher rate of interest than the ordinary share account. However, this is usually on condition that you cannot draw the money out at any time you want: some accounts require seven days' notice, other very high interest accounts require as much as 90 days or even two years! Alternatively, there may be bonus or 'gold' accounts which pay higher than normal rates of interest *and* allow you to take the money out at any time so long as you do not let your deposit fall below a certain sum (usually at least £500).

If you are able to save seriously it pays to shop around among the building societies for the best rate of interest; but if you're saving for the deposit on a house or flat and you hope to get a mortgage, keep your money with the same building society so that you build up a certain amount of goodwill.

A building society account can also act as an effective substitute for a bank account – with one major bonus: you receive interest on the money you keep in your account. Even £1 sitting in a cheque account makes money for the bank as it is money it can use, while you don't make a penny extra. Another point in favour of building societies is that most high street offices are open from 9 to 5 on weekdays and on Saturday mornings – a fact which has probably contributed to the decision of most banks to return to Saturday opening.

It pays to shop around among the building societies for the best rate of interest.

You can pay cheques into a building society account and withdraw cash either at the counter or with a cash card from the cash machines now being installed by all the bigger societies. At the moment only a few societies provide cheque books but, if you wish to make a large purchase, say for a bike or a holiday, the society will make out a cheque for you in the name of the shop or tour company. You may not – indeed you cannot – overdraw a building society account, but then, for some, this is a good discipline.

The Post Office

Aspiring savers will also find a welcome at the Post Office which is nowadays turning into something of a financial supermarket. The Post Office isn't just a place to cash your benefit cheque and buy stamps; it also offers various National Savings Schemes, like savings certificates, premium bonds, and the two National Savings accounts, the Investment and the Ordinary, and banking services through the National Girobank, which, though no longer a part of the Post Office, is administered through its branches.

Nowadays, both the banks and the building societies are required to deduct tax from the interest they pay to depositors, a deduction which you can't get back from the Inland Revenue even if you don't pay any tax. The National Savings Bank, however, is exempt from this ruling and may pay interest 'gross' – without tax being deducted. This means that if your total income from all sources (wages, benefits, interest payments) is beneath the tax threshold (see next section), you are better off saving with the NSB. Choose the Investment account which invariably pays a better rate of interest than the Ordinary, whose return is just like its name; both require £5 minimum deposit

Remember that while thrift is always said to be a virtue, you will be penalised by the DSS in the unlikely event of your claiming social security if you have savings in excess of £3,000.

Your tax

It was the American politician Benjamin Franklin (1706–90) who first pointed out that 'in this world nothing can be said to be certain except death and taxes'. Two centuries later the phrase is even more accurate, since the tax collecting system is less of a hit-and-miss affair than it was in his day.

Unless you can remain undetected in the murk of the black economy, or sail away into rock superstar tax exile, your earnings are going to be taxed.

Personal allowances

You do not have to pay tax on your whole income, since you are allowed a certain amount of income each year tax free – your 'personal allowance'. These are set each spring in the Budget by the Chancellor of the Exchequer. In 1989–90 the allowance per person was £2785. Before April 1990 wives were generally taxed under their husband's tax returns, but now both will be taxed separately and the couple will receive an additional married couple's allowance. Newspapers give the new allowances the day after the Budget, so look out for changes. You can find out your present allowance from your local tax office (look it up under Inland Revenue in the telephone book).

Tax will only be charged on the amount you earn per year above this level. Earn less than the allowance and you will not be liable for any tax at all. The allowance is least if you are a single person without dependents, and rises significantly if you're married, or have children.

If you are receiving social security there is no tax to pay on this money, but the benefits received by the unemployed (dole money plus supplementary benefit) are subject to tax. The tax is not collected until you begin work again, and is added to your tax bill for that tax year (a tax year runs from April to April).

For further details see the following Inland Revenue leaflets: IR 22 'Income Tax – Personal Allowances' and IR 29 'Income Tax and One Parent Families'.

Income tax for employees

As well as announcing the tax allowances, the Chancellor also sets out in his Budget at what rates income tax will be charged for the coming year. The basic rate paid by the majority of the working population at the time of writing is 25 per cent of income. Higher rates (40 per cent) apply to those with substantial salaries.

So long as you work for an employer rather than for yourself you will not be responsible for settling your dues to the taxman. This will be the task of your employer through the 'Pay As You Earn' (PAYE) tax scheme.

When your weekly wage exceeds £53.55 (£232 a month) your wages and salaries department will send you a form entitling them to deduct tax from your earnings. The deduction will be made on the assumption that you have no right to any other allowance other than the single person's. If you are eligible for some other allowance, such as that due to a single parent, ask the wages office for a Coding Claim form. Send this to the tax office which will assign a tax code to you taking account of the additional allowance that is owing to you. The higher the code, the less tax you will probably be paying.

Unfortunately, as an employee there are very few ways in which you can reduce the amount the Inland Revenue removes from your pay packet every week or month. For instance, though you may have bought a suit especially to wear for work – a garment which you would not dream of putting on at any other time – you are not permitted to put in a claim for this item of expenditure or any other like it.

> **66**
> **As an employee there are very few ways in which you can reduce the amount the Inland Revenue removes from your pay packet every week or month.**
> **99**

The same goes for your fare to and from work, however much the trip may cost. In addition if your boss gave you the cash to buy clothes for work or to buy a season ticket this amount would still be liable to tax. However, your company can slip you 15 pence's worth of Luncheon Vouchers daily without adding to the total tax you will be paying. Big deal!

Mortgage interest tax relief

If you have a mortgage (see p. 163), you are also given some 'tax relief' on the interest you pay back each month. This 'tax relief' used to be made through your PAYE coding so that while you gave the building society a full repayment every month, the tax office gave back some of the interest you paid out by reducing the amount of tax you had to pay. (Some people with very large mortgages or very large salaries – or both – still do it this way.) Most people now get mortgage tax relief at source (MIRAS) which means that instead of you paying less tax, your mortgage repayments are reduced instead.

As you woefully reflect that you cannot claim tax relief on rent (sorry, it's not allowed and probably never will be) cheer yourself up by looking towards the future when you may be able to exploit this mortgage allowance.

Income tax for the self-employed

If you work for yourself or run a business, you are yourself responsible for the settlement of your own tax bill – which means you must keep accurate records of your takings and outgoings, including invoices and receipts (see Self-Employed chapter). However, though you must resign yourself to hours of red tape and possible bureaucratic questioning, as a self-employed individual you have a few reasons to be cheerful.

Unlike the wage slave, you are allowed to claim for various kinds of expenses you incur in carrying out your work or business. For instance, if you work from home you can charge a proportion of your electricity, gas and phone bills, and possibly a proportion also of your rent.

Basically you will be taxed on the profit from your work – that is, your takings or total freelance income less the allowable deductions. As well as those mentioned above, these include things like advertising, postage, stationery, rent of business premises, special clothing, the cost of replacing tools, travel (including the running costs of your own car), and the interest on loans made specifically for your business.

Obviously this list is not exhaustive and some Inland Revenue offices are kinder than others to the struggling entrepreneur. Tax is a highly complex topic which provides a comfortable living for thousands of accountants and other professionals. You may not feel like making one of them any richer by taking on their services, but remember that an accountant's fee is tax-deductible and that they will know dozens of legal dodges which will save you pounds.

However, while your empire is still small, and your budget tight, you can find out all you need to know by reading the relevant chapters in the *Which? Book of Money*, published by the Consumers' Association, which should be available in your local reference library. Your tax office also offers free advice on such matters (find the address in the telephone directory under Inland Revenue). And while you are there pick up IR 28 'Starting a Business', a surprisingly readable Inland Revenue publication.

Tax avoidance – seeking legal ways of reducing your tax – is legitimate; it is tax evasion that is a criminal offence. The Inland Revenue is a mighty institution and if it suspects that you may be dealing it short it will have no hesitation in setting its considerable resources on your trail.

Student tax

Just like anybody else, a student must pay tax if his or her income exceeds the amount of the allowance. Cash from grants and other educational awards does not count as income in the taxman's eyes, though money from covenants, investment income and wages from holiday jobs is included.

The Poll Tax

Commonly known as the Poll Tax, but properly called the Community Charge, this tax was first introduced in Scotland in 1989 and was extended to the rest of the UK in 1990.

It has replaced the rates system as the method by which local authorities raise the money they need to provide the services for which they are responsible – mainly education, local roads, police, social services, public transport, the environment and planning. Although central government contributes a large amount to the cost of these through grants, local councils are responsible for collecting the rest of the money themselves and deciding how all of it should be spent. For centuries they have gained their income through the system of rates, which is a tax on property according to its value, and which was then paid by those who owned or lived in the property.

As rates were levied on property, not individuals, a household would make a single payment, irrespective of how many people lived in it. The principle behind the Poll Tax is that all adults pay it. It is pretty unlikely that your parents asked you to contribute to the rates, but now, if you are over 18 and have left school, you will find that you are the unlucky recipient of your very own annual Community Charge bill.

Although the amount varies according to the area you live in, everybody within the area pays the same.

Each local authority is responsible for raising its own tax and for setting the amount, and as different authorities have different expenditures the amount differs from borough to borough, or county to county. But although the amount varies according to the area you live in, everybody within the area pays the same, irrespective of their incomes and means. The only significant exceptions are those on low incomes and full-time students, and even they will have to pay some of the charge as the maximum rebate is 80 per cent.

Generally these are people on income support, unemployment benefit or housing benefit. If you are on one of these you should automatically be sent a form to claim a rebate by the DSS or your local authority. But if you do not get a form and you think you are eligible, write to the Community Charge Section of your local borough or district council.

Students in full-time higher education are also entitled to the full 80 per cent rebate, but you will not get one if you are only on a part-time course, unless you also qualify for income support (see 'Unemployment' chapter). You are meant to pay the tax at your main place of residence, so for students this will mean paying it in the place where they live during term time, not at their parents' home (unless these are the same). You have to send your student certificate, available from your college or university, to prove your entitlement.

The only way to avoid the community charge altogether is to become mad, go to jail, or join an order of monks or nuns – or emigrate!

VAT (Value Added Tax)

You may think that if you are not working, you are out of the tax office's reach. But don't be so sure . . . only by never making a purchase or eating a meal in a cafe or restaurant will you escape their hands. This is because you pay Value Added Tax (VAT) on almost everything you buy. The only exceptions are fuel and power (coal, gas and electricity), bus and train fares, books, maps, magazines, children's clothing, postal services, burials and cremations.

Most food is also free of VAT, but you will have to pay it on alcoholic drinks, crisps and ice cream. Nowadays VAT is also payable on restaurant meals whether you eat your biriani from a plate on the premises or from a foil dish outside.

Those items which are exempt from VAT may not always remain so. The Chancellor has the power to bring them into the VAT net whenever he wishes, though only a thick-skinned minister would be able to withstand the outcry at the imposition of the tax on clothes for children.

As well as deciding which items will be liable to VAT, the Chancellor also sets the rate of the tax in the Budget. The present 15 per cent rate has stood since 1979. VAT is also payable, at the time of writing, by self-employed people if their turnover exceeds £23,600 p.a., though this amount is normally increased each year in line with inflation. To learn more about VAT and how it works, call round at your local office of the Customs and Excise, the Government department which deals not only with duty free allowances but with VAT as well.

Borrowing money

In a perfect world no one would need to borrow. Our incomes would be sufficient to gratify all our needs and wants at once. But, since this is a pipe dream, borrowing is a fact of life. Everybody's doing it, whether you use Barclaycards or bank loans, HP or Grattan's catalogue, and unless you borrow from a kind friend or relation, it's going to cost more than the basic sum that you borrow.

The secret of agony-free borrowing is to make it work for you without letting the repayments snatch all your income. You can do this by obeying two rules. Do not borrow unless you can realistically afford the repayments. If you are earning £90 a week today, it is unlikely that you will have the earnings of a Blake Carrington in a month's time. Secondly, get the best deal you can. Do not pay over the odds if you can find cheaper elsewhere.

APR (Annual Percentage Rate)

In view of the large variety of credit deals available – bank loans, Access, Barclaycard and so on – it may seem impossible to find the best one, but in fact, all credit deals are comparable. This is because anyone offering you credit must clearly display the APR (Annual Percentage Rate) for the loan. The Annual Percentage Rate is the loan's true cost. Not only does it include the percentage interest rate payable on the loan, but reflects, for example, any arrangement fee you are required to pay for the loan, the loan period and the number and frequency of the instalments. You do not need to understand all the technicalities involved in the calculation of an APR – just to remember that the lowest APR means the least expensive credit deal.

Do not borrow on impulse. Shop around and you can make substantial savings. Let's say you have your eyes on a compact disc player. The shop will let you have the piece on hire purchase (see p. 107), but unless you are unable to get the wherewithal elsewhere, this will nearly always be the most expensive arrangement. You would be better trying to organise an overdraft at your bank since this is usually the cheapest form of borrowing because the interest charged is not as high as on most forms of loan. If your bank manager says no, ask him if you can have a personal loan – another type of borrowing which is relatively moderately priced.

The other alternative is a credit card, such as Access or Visa. You can apply for these if you are over 18. But before you fill in the form, ask yourself if you can really trust yourself with it.

Credit Cards

Access (MasterCard) and Visa are quick to point out that using their pieces of plastic can be the cheapest form of tick. But this only applies if you pay off the whole amount owing on your account by the date printed on the statement they send you each month, in which case you pay no interest at all. They require you always to pay off some of the loan, usually 5 per cent, but if you make only the minimum payment, interest becomes payable on the rest of the balance. And credit card APRs are always several percentage points higher than those payable on bank loans.

The other main credit cards, American Express and Diners Club, expect you to pay off all the sum due each month, and you have to pay to get their cards.

Every credit card customer has a credit limit which he or she must not exceed. This limit is based on the company's knowledge of your income and outgoings. Generally speaking, it is difficult to go beyond this ceiling since most retailers will contact the credit card company for authorisation before letting you take the goods away – but it is possible.

In such circumstances the credit card company will often offer to raise your limit – but this is an inducement to spend you can do without. Be wary of raising a loan on your card – repaying both this advance and other purchases on the card may be too much for your budget.

If you are sensible you should be able to play one card wisely, never letting the credit card company make too much money out of you by allowing an overdue balance to run and run for months. If you are tempted to put in for another from a rival company, try to stand firm. Muse on the fate of the couple who landed up in bankruptcy court with £32,000 worth of debts incurred by juggling 52 credit cards. After all, they must have started somewhere. Some of those wretched pieces of plastic were store credit cards now available from shops large and small. When visiting a store you cannot help but notice the leaflets inviting you to apply usually displayed at the checkout, or even slipped into the bag containing your purchase.

All retailers would prefer you to use their in-store cards because they have to pay the national credit card companies a levy of between 1 and 4 per cent of the price of the goods every time they accept payment with one. It's much more profitable for them to give you credit themselves – they don't pay a levy and they can earn interest if you can't pay up immediately you get the bill. However, store credit cards almost invariably charge higher APRs. To make things more complex, retailers may soon charge customers a higher price for goods bought with a non-store credit card than with cash or a cheque. If you are faced with this the arithmetic of working out whether a store card would be cheaper would become quite complex.

Banks are now encouraging us to use debit cards. The biggest two are Connect (Barclays) and Switch (NatWest). They operate as a cross between a credit card and a cheque: they look like credit cards, but the sum spent is immediately deducted from your account.

Hire Purchase (HP)

In-store credit cards are a fairly recent innovation; before they got on to this ruse, stores and finance companies were gleaning fat pickings from another source of credit – hire purchase.

'HP' should always be your final borrowing choice simply because it is almost certainly the most expensive. Not for nothing did it earn the title 'buying on the never-never'! However, if you must opt for this exorbitant alternative, visit several shops all stocking the same type of goods. HP APRs are bound to vary among the various car showrooms and hi-fi superstores. And before you sign on the dotted line of an HP agreement, make sure you are aware of what you are letting yourself in for. You usually have to be over 18 to buy on HP.

Hire purchase means just what it says. You are hiring the goods from the seller and you will not own them until you have paid the last instalment. If you fail to pay, the shop (or the finance company that's backing the loan) can come around to take the goods back. However, if you have paid off more than a third of the amount the lenders have by law to take out a court order before they can knock on your door. (This regulation applies only if the motorbike or whatever cost less than £7,500.) If you sign in haste and repent later at your leisure, it is not a disaster because the law also allows you a five day period in which you can extract yourself from the agreement.

Occasionally you will find that the hire purchase company requires you to give the name of another person who will stand 'guarantor' for your debt. This individual must guarantee to pay what you owe if you default on your payments at some time in the future. He or she must come up with the cash – regardless of his or her financial situation. This is a considerable undertaking which can strain friendship to the limit. Think twice before asking someone else to fulfil this role for you and avoid the responsibility if someone asks you to act as a guarantor.

Finance Houses

When you enter into a hire purchase agreement, the credit is frequently extended to you not by the shop where you buy the goods but by a finance company acting in association with the retailer.

These are reputable organisations, governed, like the banks, by a wealth of legislation. This does not however make them the cheapest source of cash if you want a loan to tide you over. Do not borrow from a finance company unless your bank has turned you down.

Catalogues

You may wonder why so many people who could easily get to the shops prefer to buy from catalogues. One reason is that the mail order firms give free credit. Send away for something and you can usually enjoy free credit for 20 weeks, or longer if the item costs more. Make sure, however, that you cannot buy cheaper elsewhere.

Loan sharks

All the forms of borrowing discussed come within the law and are governed by strict regulations. However, there are many other shady organisations willing to offer credit – at a price. These are the back street moneylenders – the loan sharks – a breed that has existed for as long as man has been unable to make ends meet. They prey on the hard-up of all ages but have a taste for catching their customers young. A favourite quarry is the young single mother unable to manage on her benefit money and lacking the credentials or the know-how to borrow elsewhere.

Never take money from a loan shark. Not only will he charge an astronomical APR, he may also resort to heavy-handed tactics if you cannot meet your obligations.

If someone calls at the houses in your street, hawking loans, he is breaking the law. When he rings your bell, ask him outright if he has a licence to lend. This will ensure his swift departure, but before he slips away take a mental note of his 'trading' name and appearance and report him to the police – he may have ensnared a neighbour.

Never take money from a loan shark.

If you have unfortunately already borrowed from a shark, of the sharp-suited variety, ask for advice at the Citizens Advice Bureau, who will be able to put you in touch with your local trading standards office. This is part of the Office of Fair Trading, the offical arrangements body that regulates credit. They will be able to pursue the loan shark and can also help you get to grips with your debts in some other way.

In trouble

Since the average Briton owes an amount equal to a year's pay, it is not surprising that, from time to time, individuals can encounter difficulties in repaying their loans.

If you are finding it hard to keep up with your payments, it is wise to inform the lender as soon as possible. If you cannot pay back the whole amount required each month, see if they will accept a lesser amount – any arrangement in fact that will keep the case out of the courts. You do not want to risk having an order made against you for the debt which will endanger your future ability to get credit.

Do not be tempted to take out another loan to get you out of your fix. Rather make an appointment at your local Citizens Advice Bureau or Consumers' Advice Centre. The counsellor will need to know everything about your income and expenditure but don't hold back – you may find that he or she can actually find ways to *increase* your income. It could be that you are not claiming benefits that are your due, or that you are being over-taxed.

Consumer rights

You may have thought that contracts were the preserve of lawyers but unwittingly you have yourself been entering into contracts for as long as you can remember . . .

Each time you buy something in a shop, however small, you are party to a contract – an agreement under which both you and the shopkeeper enjoy rights. Essentially you have the right to purchase an item that is of 'merchantable quality' and 'fit for the purpose' for which it is being supplied.

This means that if your new shoes fall apart the first time you step out in them you deserve a refund – so long as any fault in the shoes was not pointed out to you at the time of purchase. Do not worry if you lost your receipt. Though the shop may insist that you need this slip of paper to claim your cash back, this assertion has no backing in law.

You can accept a credit note instead of the cash but only if this suits you. However, if you are returning the shoes simply because they make your legs look unattractive or because the colour clashes with your trousers, take a credit note willingly and say thank you, because in such cases the shop is not obliged to take back the goods.

Your rights to take goods back if they are faulty apply also during sale time, though notices posted in shops can often suggest that this is not the case. If you spot a sign saying 'no refunds' and you are refused your money back, take the matter to the local trading standards officer (telephone your local authority to find him or her) – such signs are illegal.

Second-hand goods bought from a shop or dealer are also subject to the various consumer acts but if you buy something from a friend you have little or no redress if the object is faulty.

If a shop proves difficult over a purchase that you regard as substandard, do not pick a quarrel with the assistant. Write to the managing director, outlining your complaint. If you hear nothing, seek the help of your Citizens Advice Bureau or the local trading standards officer.

Insurance

Buy the papers every day for a week or switch on the TV every evening and during that time you are bound to read or hear something about the 'rising tide of burglaries'. This is not just journalism. The number of thefts and break-ins has increased significantly – a phenomenon which has produced something of a siege mentality among the older generation. Some semis nowadays resemble fortresses, bristling with bars, bolts and locks.

Though it is unnecessary to go to such lengths, if you want to protect your worldly goods (however few they may be) give a thought to a good lock on the front door of your home or room. But bear in mind that locks only slow a thief down, they do not stop him. So think about some insurance. It need not be expensive to cover your belongings against theft, fire, loss or damage.

Insuring your property is usually done through an insurance broker, who will arrange an insurance policy for you with one of the big insurance companies. You can find insurance brokers in the Yellow Pages or other local business directories – it's worth ringing round to get the best deal. And make sure you know which company they are placing your policy with. Ask friends or family who have already got insurance for recommendations, or try the Citizens Advice Bureau. Alternatively you can apply direct to the insurance companies themselves.

When you are working out what your property is worth, be realistic. Your mum may have given you that camera three years ago – do you really know how much it would cost to replace it if it's stolen? You may have been building up your record collection for years – what's it going to cost to replace them if they go up in smoke?

Insurance is usually worked out on a 'new for old' basis – that is, on the cost of replacing an old item with a brand new one. There are some exceptions (clothes and household linen are important ones), but the company will let you know. With an 'all risks' policy – for which you pay a higher premium of course – you can get insurance for a certain amount of cash, for credit cards, and things like cameras or musical instruments which may well be lost or stolen outside your home. Many companies won't pay up on small claims, though – for instance, the first £50 of any claim may have to be covered by you. So check your policy *before* you pay the premium. And don't forget, it's illegal to drive a car if it's uninsured.

It may be difficult to fit an insurance premium into an already restricted budget, but it's worth considering it as a necessary expense. Some brokers – the Endsleigh and the Oxford-based Harrison Beaumont for instance – offer policies especially designed for students or nurses living away from home. If you rent or own a flat or house and have even a few sticks of furniture to call your own and a few valuables, you need a fully fledged house contents policy.

Making a claim

If something is lost, stolen, damaged or destroyed by fire, make a claim as soon as possible. Telephone your broker or insurance company, tell them you want to make a claim and they will send you a form to fill in. In the case of theft you must inform the police – and the insurance company probably won't pay up until they are sure every effort has been made to recover your property. If your claim is turned down, or only paid in part, ask the company for the reason at once. Otherwise go to the Citizens Advice Bureau or get in touch direct with the Insurance Ombudsman (whose job is to look into disputed claims) or the Personal Insurance Arbitration Service (addresses on p. 241).

Life Insurance

This is not something you will probably be thinking about at this stage, although it's worth doing if you get a mortgage and are married or have children. One thing to remember about life insurance while you are still young is that it is very cheap!

P|OLITICS

Britain has one of the oldest democracies in the world. The system we have today has evolved over the centuries, and is based on one person, one vote. This means that at certain intervals the people of the country can change their national or local government if they are dissatisfied with the ruling party, and elect another.

Because of this long evolution of our forms of government the terms and procedures followed, especially in Parliament, can seem somewhat obscure and difficult to understand, but it is worth getting to grips with them if you really want to know how the decisions that affect all of us are made, and how to influence them.

But even if you do not wish to understand fully the complexities of government, you are not in a position to complain about how things are run if you do not use your vote, and understand what it is that you are voting for. Much is made of the power of this vote, and although your single cross may seem very isolated and lonely, when gathered and counted with those of the same opinion as you, it can have a massive effect. Even if the person or party you voted for isn't elected, the number of votes they gained can often temper the decisions of those who are.

The Vote

On your eighteenth birthday you become entitled to vote in elections. Each October a form is delivered to every household on which is to be entered the details of each person in the house aged 18 and over or who will be 18 in the next year. These forms are used to draw up the electoral roll, which lists all people who are entitled to vote in that area. First a draft document is published, which you can check in local libraries or at the council offices. If your name is omitted, contact the electoral registration officer immediately at your council offices. The final roll is available the following February.

Elections come in three forms: national, local and for the European Parliament. In a national election the entire nation votes, and as a result the government can be changed, or re-elected with a larger or smaller majority in the House of Commons; local elections are held for local councils, when the residents in the area administered by that council can elect a new one. Occasionally an MP or councillor will die or resign, in which case a by-election is held to replace him or her.

Very occasionally the electorate is asked to vote in a referendum. These are held when the government wants to gauge public opinion on a specific issue. The only national one ever was in 1975, on whether Britain should leave the Common Market or not, and two regional ones were held in 1979 over the devolution of power to Scotland and Wales. Each member of the electorate is asked to say yes or no to a simple question, but the government is in no way legally bound to act on the result.

Just before any election you will receive a polling card through the post. This will tell you when and where to vote. If you are to be away from home when an election is taking place, or are unable to get to the polling station because of a physical disability, you are entitled to a postal vote or a proxy vote, under which you authorise another person to cast your vote for you. The electoral registration office will explain the procedures.

But if you can vote normally, you go along to the polling station indicated on the card, which will be near your home. You do not need to take the card with you, but if you do it will speed up the issuing of the voting slip; otherwise just give your name and address to the person issuing the slips when you get there. You take your slip into a booth, mark an 'X' by the candidate (or candidates in some elections) of your choice, put the slip in the famous battered black metal box, and that's it – you're part of Britain's democracy!

Parliament

The constitution of the United Kingdom is not contained in any single document, as in many other countries such as the USA, but is made up of statute, common law and convention. It can be changed by Act of Parliament and is thus felt to be more adaptable to changes in political climate.

Parliament is the law-making authority of the UK, and is made up of three parts – the Queen, the House of Lords and the House of Commons. Although they are each constituted differently and meet together only on specific occasions, they all have to 'agree' at the end of the day in order for the law-making process to take place. The main functions of Parliament are to pass laws (which cannot afterwards be disputed in a court of law but are often 'interpreted'), provide the means by which government can carry out its work, and scrutinise government policy and administration.

Each Parliament lasts a maximum of five years but can be dissolved and elections for a new Parliament called before the end of its term. Its life is subdivided into sessions, each of which lasts a year, beginning in October or November. There are various adjournments, or holidays, throughout the year, which means that the Commons meets, or 'sits', on average 175 days per year, the Lords 150 days.

The Queen is Head of State and largely performs a figurehead role, although the decision to summon or dissolve Parliament is technically hers. At the start of each session of Parliament she delivers a speech known as the Queen's Speech. This is, in fact, written by the government, and outlines its broad policies and proposed programme for the session. The Queen also has to give Royal Assent to each Bill passed by Parliament; appoint the Prime Minister; appoint certain key officers including judges, bishops, diplomats; and confer honours (knights, MBEs etc). She also has the power to remit all or part of a sentence of a convicted person. However, here she never acts on personal whim, but is advised by government ministers or follows precedent.

115

At present the House of Commons comprises 650 members elected by voters arranged into constituencies. These constituencies average 67,000 voters each and are drawn up by four Boundary Commissions, each of which reviews its specific area periodically to monitor population shifts. Voting is optional and secret and by single, non-transferable vote, which means that each person has one vote, and the candidate with most votes is elected. In Euro-elections in Northern Ireland there is a system of proportional representation, whereby voters list the candidates in order of preference.

Almost any person who is a citizen of Britain, the Republic of Ireland or the Commonwealth, is resident in the UK and is over 21 may stand for election. The only people who are disqualified are undischarged bankrupts, members of the clergy, peers, members of the police and armed forces, or those who have served a prison sentence of over a year. A candidate has to be proposed and seconded by two electors registered in the constituency and backed by eight others. He or she must put up a deposit of £1,000 which is forfeited if he or she receives five per cent or less of the votes cast in that constituency.

> **66**
>
> **The 20 most important ministers form the Cabinet, which is responsible for the final determination of policy and the co-ordination of the various government departments.**
>
> **99**

The Prime Minister is appointed by the Queen from the party gaining the overall majority of seats at a general election. All other ministers are appointed by the Queen on the recommendation of the Prime Minister. The 20 most important ministers form the Cabinet, which is responsible for the final determination of policy and the co-ordination of the various government departments. It meets in private and its proceedings are confidential, being governed by the Official Secrets Act, which means that Cabinet papers can only be made public after a time lapse of 30 years, and then only with the approval of the government in office.

Members of the House of Lords are not elected, but are either appointed by the Queen on the Prime Minister's advice, or have inherited their peerage ('hereditary peers') and are over 21. The Lords also contains 26 archbishops and bishops, and the Lords of Appeal, or 'Law Lords', who represent the final court of appeal for civil cases in Britain and for criminal cases in England, Wales and Northern Ireland (see p. 140). Lords receive no salary as such, only attendance and travelling expenses. They align themselves with either the government or the opposition party or sit on the cross-benches. The House is presided over by the Lord Chancellor.

Acts of Parliament

The main legislative function of Parliament is the drafting, debating and passing of Bills. They can be introduced in either House by either a government minister (in which case they are called 'public Bills') or by an ordinary MP, but the most usual position for them is to be introduced by the government in the House of Commons. Before a public Bill even gets to be presented for debate, considerable consultation goes on with interested parties on the specific subject matter, resulting in a White Paper which outlines proposals for legislative changes which may be presented for debate in a Bill. Sometimes Green Papers are issued before White Papers; these are consultative documents which outline proposals still at a formative stage, in order to promote public discussion.

When a Bill is initially introduced into Parliament, it receives what is known as the First Reading, a formality to coincide with its printing but at which there is no debate. At the Second Reading there is a major debate on the Bill in the House of Commons. It is then referred to a Standing Committee, made up of between 16 and 50 members selected to reflect the overall

117

strength of the political parties, who give the Bill detailed examination. This is the point at which amendments can start to be made, and concessions agreed between the parties. The Report Stage sees the Standing Committee report back to the House and take further amendments. In the Third Reading, the Bill is reviewed in its final form – this stage can be passed without debate unless six MPs put forward a motion to the contrary. Then, if the Bill has been introduced in the Commons it goes to the House of Lords where it goes through broadly the same stages, and *vice versa* for a Bill introduced in the Lords. After a Bill has passed all stages it goes to the Queen for Royal Assent (which is never refused) and then becomes an Act of Parliament. So, although they're separate, the two Houses must agree proposed legislation for it to become law.

Bills of a controversial nature invariably are introduced in the Commons and pass to the Lords. Those of a less controversial nature often start in the Lords and go to the Commons. As we have an elective democracy, the Commons is much more powerful than the Lords, so it is most unlikely that the Lords would prevent a Bill passed by the Commons from becoming law. However, it may amend it and return it to the Commons for consideration. On the other hand, if a Bill originating in the Lords proved unacceptable to the Commons it would be unlikely to become law as no debating time would be given to it.

Bills tabled by individual MPs are known as Private Members' Bills. At the start of each session members ballot against each other to introduce a Bill on one of the Fridays set aside specifically for this. Only 20 are taken each session and few succeed in becoming law. They are subject to the same parliamentary procedure as public Bills. Private Members' Bills can also be introduced in the Lords. Members can also try to get a Bill introduced through the 'ten minute rule' in the Commons, under which two speeches, one for, one against a measure are allowed, and then the House decides whether to allow the Bill to be introduced properly.

Other Parliamentary Procedures

The House of Commons also has 14 Select Committees. These are set up to give closer scrutiny to government departments, policies and ministerial conduct. They are formed on a party basis, and reflect party strength in the House. They conduct hearings on specific matters which the public is entitled to attend, and publish reports. In theory they provide MPs with a monitoring service on the government's activities. In practice, the government is under no obligation to take any notice of their findings and a recent survey found that only about three per cent of Select Committee reports are debated. They do, however, often get reported in the media and thus serve to bring some influence to bear on both the public and MPs.

In addition to the work of Select Committees, there are some other occasions when government policy can be questioned. These include Question Time, an hour set aside each day from Monday to Thursday when ministers answer MPs' questions and information can be elicited; MPs can use a half-hour adjournment period at the end of each day to bring up matters of specific public or constituency concern; and there are 19 opposition days each session when the opposition chooses the subject for debate.

A Whip is the name given to the people appointed by each of the main parliamentary parties to ensure attendance by as many members as possible for a particularly important debate or vote. The letter issued by them to members is also known as the whip, and the urgency of the matter in hand is denoted by the number of times the item is underlined. Failure to turn up in the House at the summons of a 'three-line' whip usually means disciplinary proceedings within the party.

A publication called *Hansard* gives verbatim reports of speeches and written answers in each House. It is published by Her Majesty's Stationery Office and appears daily while Parliament is sitting. The Public Information Office (071-219 4272) is a useful place to contact for any query relating to the work, proceedings and history of the House of Commons. The Journal and Information Office (071-219 3107) provides the same service for the House of Lords.

Access to Parliament

The proceedings of both Houses are open to the public, except on rare occasions. Normal sitting hours are 2.30 pm to 10.30 pm Monday to Thursday, and from 9.30 am to 3.00 pm on Fridays. You can queue up to sit in the public gallery, but it's a better idea to approach your MP for a ticket in advance.

> **66**
>
> ## Don't forget that your local MP is there to work for you.
>
> **99**

Don't be put off by all the parliamentary jargon. The Bills going through Parliament will, of course, reflect the policies of the parties in power and will have been outlined in that party's election manifesto, but you can make your views on Bills known by making submissions at certain stages of its passage and by lobbying your MP and discussing his or her voting intentions on it in Parliament (you can also write to members of the House of Lords about Bills too). Don't be intimidated by what may appear to be a massive institution – there are ways to make your voice heard.

And don't forget that your local MP is there to work for you, whether you voted for him or her or not. As at January 1990, an MP's salary stands at £26,701 basic, plus around £24,000 secretarial/research expenses, plus additional travel expenses (a Cabinet minister's basic is £55,220) – so don't be shy about contacting him or her to find out information for you, to ask a Parliamentary Question on an issue, and even approach ministers. Every constituent has the right to visit the House of Commons and when there to send in a 'Green Card' asking to see his or her MP. However, it is generally far more advisable to write beforehand (an MP is obliged to reply to all letters sent to the constituency address) or go for an initial appointment at the local party office, where the MP will be available on a regular basis (known as a surgery), say one day a week or a fortnight. Your library should be able to tell you where the surgery is and when it's open.

Political parties

The party which wins the most seats in the House of Commons forms the government. This has resulted in a predominantly two-party system, with the government being formed by either the Conservative Party or the Labour Party for most of this century.

The Conservatives trace their origins to the eighteenth century and the Labour Party to the last decade of the nineteenth century. The former Liberal Party has its roots in the eighteenth century, but last formed a government on its own in 1906–16. The Social Democratic Party (SDP) was set up in 1981 and then merged in 1988 with the Liberals to form the Social and Liberal Democrats (which has since changed its name to the Liberal Democrats), but various members of the SDP kept going as a separate party under David Owen. The most recent arrival on the political scene, though with no MPs from the 1987 election, is the Green Party. Formed in the 1970s its main concern is how we should organize our lives to preserve the environment.

Other parties with elected members to Parliament are the nationalist parties: Plaid Cymru (formed in Wales, 1925); the Scottish National Party (1934); and from Northern Ireland, the Democratic Unionist Party, the Ulster Unionist Party, the nationalist Socialist Democratic and Labour Party (SDLP), and Sinn Fein (who, while recently taking up many seats on local councils, have a policy of abstaining from Westminster).

The main addresses of these parties are given on p. 243, but they do of course have branches all over the country and their HQ will give you details of your nearest local party office.

If you wish to become active in politics beyond just casting your vote in elections you can join the major political party of your choice. You apply for membership by contacting the head office or the local branch (address available from your nearest library). Provided you are accepted into membership, you are entitled to attend local meetings. These are usually held monthly and discuss national and local issues, the selection of council and parliamentary candidates and fund-raising matters. The branch is run by elected officers (chair, secretary, treasurer), and, as well as the general monthly meetings, the branch elects committees to meet and discuss areas such as finance and policy. These committees report back to the general meeting which is the sovereign body of the party. The Labour Party branches also usually have women's committees and, in some areas, black committees. The Conservative Party also has its own women's groups. Local parties may also have 'interest' groupings that campaign on specific issues.

All parties have youth sections which you can join (membership is not mandatory as you can just join the party like any other member), and which discuss issues specific to younger people. Policies and decisions are often passed on to the main branch or party for possible adoption. The youth groups are inevitably more 'radical' than the main party, whether of the right or left, and have been known to incur the leader's wrath. They also organise socials and the like, so are an excellent opportunity to make new friends.

Each of the political parties hold annual national conferences attended by branch delegates (apart from the Greens, whose conference is at the time of writing open to any member who wishes to attend). These debate and vote on motions, most of which have originated in branches, to decide or advise on the future policy of the party and its practical progress; delegate election varies from party to party but once you've joined and become active, you can stand for election. The main parties also hold youth section conferences and some hold special interest conferences as well.

Other political groups

'Non-party politics' covers a massive range, both in number and political aspirations, of political organisations, pressure groups and bodies outside the mainstream of Parliamentary parties and local government. These can broadly be divided into two categories.

First, there are various groups to the right and left of the parliamentary parties that pursue a wide range of radical politics. These range from, on the left, the Workers' Revolutionary Party, a fundamentalist Trotskyist group, the Socialist Workers' Party, a more populist Trotskyist group with a strong Midlands industrial base, and the Communist Party of Great Britain (Marxist-Leninist) which follows the doctrines of Chairman Mao; to the extreme right with neo-Fascist groups like the National Front or the British Movement, whose main platform is racial discrimination and whose members have allegedly been involved with racial attacks on the property and persons of members of this country's multi-ethnic society.

Between these two extremes are other groups which still have a strong political colour, such as the Freedom Association and AIMS on the right, and the Communist Party on the left, which campaigns for radical change but also puts up candidates at local and national elections. Numerous other parties are active on a broad range of issues including women's rights, trade union reform and the British presence in Northern Ireland, and it's no exaggeration to say that, if you are interested in more radical policies than those presented by the Parliamentary parties, a party exists that will appeal to you.

However, one word of caution. Before joining any party read its literature, try and find an independent source of information about it, ask if you can attend a meeting without obligation, and resist all blandishments and flattery to join up until you're really sure and ready. Like love at first sight, later realities can be a painful experience.

The other category of non-party political groups are those that concentrate on one or a very small number of specific issues. Again, the spectrum is massively wide. The best-known are probably the Campaign for Nuclear Disarmament (CND), which is concerned with ridding the world of nuclear weapons through pressure on Parliament, education, demonstrations, meetings and media coverage, and Friends of the Earth, who campaign to prevent the further erosion of the natural environment. The Animal Liberation Front is committed to ending abuse of animals by rescuing them from factory farms and laboratories and inflicting economic damage through sabotage on the industries that it considers abuse animals. The Wages for Housework Campaign lobbies for recognition that women's unpaid work is a significant input to the national economy. These are national campaigns, although membership varies. At a local level, there are groups that campaign for the unemployed, women, gay men and lesbians, and members of the ethnic groups. Local communities sometimes band together to fight a specific cause, such as stopping a motorway being built through the countryside or the closure of a hospital.

The list and range is almost endless, and if you are specifically interested in one area of change through political activity, there is a local or national group that shares your concern and would welcome your help – once again, check them out, although these groups are pretty 'open' in their aims.

Getting in touch with a group which is engaged in an area of activity you're interested in depends on their size and where you live. Your local library should be able to tell you where to find the local section of large groups like Greenpeace or CND, or at least give you the national office address, and you should also check your local paper for details of meetings. If you live in an urban area, and even in some rural areas, there is often an 'alternative' magazine or newspaper with such information in it.

However, if you live in the country, it is often harder to find such groups, particularly if they are relatively small. You could try ringing the news reporter on your local newspaper – he or she may have come across them in the past and have a phone number. You could also try the local major political parties, who may have had contact with or be involved in such areas. The student union or local trades unions may also have information. If all else fails, write to the National Council for Voluntary Organisations, 26 Bedford Square, London WC1, or the British Youth Council, 57 Chalton Street, London NW1. Both organisations should be able to refer you to groups that share similar interests to yours.

Politics isn't just about meetings and resolutions but drinks afterwards, getting together, meeting people with similar interests to yours and often broadening your own.

A final word of advice. While you may only pay the subscription and receive literature through the post, real involvement with and commitment to any form of politics means regularly attending meetings, campaigning, voluntary work and speaking and writing, and can be exhausting and take up a lot of your free time. On the other hand, it can be a lot of fun, rewarding and a valuable part of your social life – politics isn't just about meetings and resolutions but drinks afterwards, getting together, meeting people with similar interests to yours and often broadening your own.

Local government

The level below national government is local government, which can largely be broken into two sections.

The metropolitan authorities and non-metropolitan counties were abolished in the mid-1980s and replaced by appointed bodies with many of their functions such as education and health provisions and transport policy becoming the responsibility of local councils.

A local council's task is to be responsible for the practical sides of public life in line with both national and local policy. For example, it is responsible for libraries, roads, local planning and housing, parks and recreation.

Mainly in rural areas, there are also parish councils, which deal with matters such as allotments, community halls and local planning.

Local council services are funded in two ways. National government grants them money from central funds, and the council itself levies money from all resident adults and commercial property-owners in the council area. The latter pay what is known as the 'business rate', while individuals pay the community charge, commonly known as the poll tax (see 'Money matters' chapter).

Elections for councillors are held every four years. Just as for parliamentary elections the country is divided into constituencies, the area covered by a local council is divided up into 'wards', each one of which elects a councillor or councillors to represent it.

If your dustbin hasn't been emptied for a month or the local library is closing early because of staffing cuts, it's the local council you contact to complain. For practical problems, contact the relevant department listed under the council's name in the phone book, but for matters of policy, contact your local councillor or councillors. The Town Hall will tell you who they are, and because they operate at a more grass-roots level than MPs, you can usually ring them or they will come round to see you (most also hold surgeries – see p. 121).

Councillors are usually local people and anyone can stand for election. Although it is usually the main parties' candidates who are elected, more independent councillors are elected nationally than independent MPs, especially in rural areas. Councillors receive no salary but can claim attendance expenses for council meetings. These are open to the public (as are most council committee meetings) – ask your Town Hall for details.

Local councillors are responsible to national government but also, more importantly, to the local people who elected them. You should get their support on reasonable requests to the council, such as having a crossing installed near a school or improving street-lighting, and they should take into account local wishes on policy matters affecting the area.

The European Parliament

The European Parliament is the policy-making body of the European Community (EC), or Common Market as it is usually known. It has 434 elected members (MEPs), 81 of whom are British. Obviously, constituencies are much larger than for national elections, and may not directly reflect the political bias of some of the areas within them, but they are relevant to people in Britain. The Parliament is mainly concerned in shaping European legislation, which in turn affects British law. It has various committees whose functions cover a wide range of EC interests; there is also Question Time, as at Westminster, and you can ask your MEP to put down a question by writing to him or her at the constituency address (ask at your local library).

[T]HE LAW

What is the law for?

Imagine a country with no traffic lights or speed limits. Great! Forget the Isle of Man TT, forget the Monte Carlo Rally, you could turn your own back street into a race track. Or could you? What if you came to a cross roads and no one wanted to give way? What if you knocked over some children crossing the road?

In any group people have rights. But when my right to drive as fast as I like affects your right to cross the road, it becomes a responsibility. Other people's rights are your responsibilities.

The law is a set of rights and responsibilities allowing people to co-exist without unnecessary interference. If you step on someone else's toe – or infringe their legal right – then they have the right to take you to court. That is their remedy.

In the USA it is easy to see what your rights are because the rules and regulations are contained in a written Constitution or Bill of Rights. In this country there is no written Constitution or Bill of Rights. How then do you know what your rights are?

To get the right answer every time, you will probably have to ask a lawyer, and a good one at that, or else become one yourself. The fact is that there are no easy answers. You almost have to look at everything that you *can't* do and then see what's left.

Take freedom of speech, for example. You can't just come out and say what you like, where you like, and about whom you like. If you threaten or insult someone or swear at them in public, that could be a criminal offence. Incitement to racial hatred is a criminal offence. So is publishing obscene material. Talking about material classified as confidential could be a breach of the

Official Secrets Act. If you lie about someone in such a way as to damage their reputation, you could be breaking the libel laws. So in all these cases the laws that exist to protect the rights of others limit your freedom of speech. Where your freedom of speech ends, your responsibility to others begins.

Laws are made by Parliament (see previous chapter) and are interpreted by judges in the courts. A decision by a judge in one case creates a precedent for future cases, and in this way a body of case law has been built up over the centuries. But if Parliament makes the law, why does it need to be interpreted by judges? The reason is that individual words and phrases can often mean different things when applied to different sets of facts – all the more so when clever lawyers with a living to earn can persuade you that black is white and white is black (or at least dark grey).

Citizens' Rights

Providing that you are not obviously breaking the criminal law, you are generally free to do what you want, although there are some limitations. Mostly these restrictions apply to group activity. There is, for example, no specific right to hold a public meeting, and it is usually wise to inform the police if you plan to do so. Neither is there a right to demonstrate in public, although you are generally allowed to. You do have the legal right to demonstrate outside your workplace in furtherance of an industrial dispute, but there is no specific legal right if the picket is for a political purpose, such as outside an embassy.

You have to bear in mind the limitations placed on you by the rights of others in all these cases. While picketing your place of work you are not allowed to block the road, or shout abuse at other people. And if you are planning a demonstration the police have the powers to regulate the route of the march – or even stop it altogether – if they think it is likely to end in trouble.

One important new set of specific rights is to be free of harassment or discrimination on account of your race or sex.

Your Age and your Rights

Between the ages of 16 and 21 you gain different legal rights. Here are the most notable ones.

16

You can leave school.

You can leave home with your parents' consent.

You can get married in Scotland.

You can get married with your parents' consent in the rest of the UK.

You can consent to sexual intercourse, except in Northern Ireland.

You can have a full-time job.

You can claim supplementary benefit.

You can consent to medical treatment.

You can drive a moped.

You can buy cigarettes and tobacco.

You can have wine, beer or cider with a meal in a restaurant.

17

You can consent to sexual intercourse in Northern Ireland.

You can be imprisoned.

You can drive most vehicles apart from goods vehicles.

You can become a street trader.

18

You reach the age of majority (official adulthood).

You can vote.

You can drive a medium-sized vehicle.

You can bet.

You can buy alcohol.

You can see an adults-only film or buy an adults-only video.

21

You can become an MP or a local councillor.

A man can consent to a homosexual act, providing his partner is over 21.

You can drive a large passenger or heavy goods vehicle.

Police powers and your rights

On 1 January 1986 a far-reaching law, the Police and Criminal Evidence Act, came into force. This gave the police new powers in the areas of stop and search, arrest and detention. It was also supposed to provide the citizen with extra safeguards against the misuse by the police of their new powers, but at the time it was widely criticised for extending these powers too far, and many people are still unhappy with it.

The police can stop and search you or your car in public if they have reason to believe that you are carrying either stolen goods or what are called 'prohibited articles'. While these include obviously offensive weapons like flick-knives, they could also be quite harmless objects, such as a comb, a bunch of keys, a credit card, a pencil or a coin, if the police think you are going to use the object to injure someone or for theft, burglary or deception.

However, the police cannot stop and search you just because of your colour or the way you look, nor because they know you have been to court before for possession of an unlawful article.

If you are stopped, you should never be asked to take off more than a coat, jacket or gloves in public. Any more thorough search must be 'out of public view' and be carried out by someone of the same sex as yourself. The police must also tell you their names and police station, the reason they have stopped you and what they are looking for, and must make a record of the search and inform you of your right to a copy.

What to do if arrested

Only about one in 60,000 young people gets into serious trouble with the police, but if you are 'helping the police with their enquiries', it will normally be because you are one of that tiny minority to have been arrested. Nobody has to go to a police station unless arrested, and the police have to tell you (a) that you are under arrest, and (b) what the reason for the arrest is. If they do not, the arrest is unlawful. If you are only in a police station because you have been asked to go and have not been charged with any crime, you are free to leave whenever you wish, although you may find yourself pressured to stay.

Being arrested, especially for the first time, is almost always a frightening and unpleasant experience. If you are innocent, you may feel angry and be inclined to show it. If guilty, you may be overtaken by panic at what could happen to you. In either case, the important thing to remember is to stay calm and not to lose your temper. Due deference to the police is usually the best policy. This does not mean licking their boots but simply being polite. Whether you are innocent or guilty, this kind of attitude is more likely to result in your prompt release from police hands.

The new law gives the police such vastly increased powers of arrest that it's simply not going to be worth arguing whether the arrest was unlawful or not until you have had legal advice. And the same goes for being searched on arrest.

Nobody has to go to a police station unless arrested.

Once you have been arrested, the police have to take you to a police station as soon as possible. Once there, they should inform you of your right to contact a friend or relative, and also of your right to get in touch with a solicitor. If you do not know a solicitor, there will be one on standby, called the Duty Solicitor, whom you can telephone and ask to come and see you. There is also a list of solicitors kept in the Charge Room which you can consult if for any reason you do not want to see the Duty Solicitor.

You cannot normally be kept at a police station for longer than 24 hours, but you can be kept for up to 36 hours if you are accused of committing a particularly serious offence. If the police have a very good reason for wanting to keep you inside even longer – for example, if you might tip someone off about the location of some stolen property – they can go to a magistrate for the necessary authority to keep you in custody.

Once the police have enough evidence against you, they should charge you by writing out the offence on a charge sheet and cautioning you. The magic words are: 'You do not have to say anything unless you wish to do so, but what you say may be given in evidence.' From the moment you are arrested until you are charged and after, you have the right not to answer any questions or to make a statement, whether innocent or not.

It is usually best not to make any kind of statement until you have had legal advice. If you do wish to make a statement, however, it is always advisable to keep it simple, for example, if accused of stealing an apple, do not say, 'I don't like apples and anyway I was in New York at the time,' simply say, 'I didn't steal that apple'.

Unless the police have good reason to keep you in custody, after you have been charged you will be released on bail. This means that you will have to appear at a magistrate's or juvenile court at a time specified by the police.

If you are under 17, the police must take special steps to find out who is looking after you. They have to tell them about the arrest, the reason for it and where you are being held. They should not interview you or take a written statement from you unless there is an adult present. If you are on a Supervision Order, they must inform your supervisor. If in care, they must tell the local authority or organisation with parental rights. The police must ask the person who is responsible for you to come to the station to see you and they must give you the right to contact a friend or relative, although this can be delayed in the case of a particularly serious offence.

You can be searched after arrest, but only if the police believe you have evidence of an offence, or something you could use to escape or injure someone with. You can be strip-searched, but only by an officer of the same sex and with no one else present except a doctor. The police can also do an 'intimate search' if a senior officer thinks you have something hidden on you, such as a Class A drug (for example heroin), or an item which could cause injury. An 'intimate search' of a body orifice must only be done by a doctor or nurse at a hospital or doctor's surgery, except in emergency.

The courts

'Trespassers will be prosecuted' it often says, but will they? The answer is no, because a trespasser has not committed a crime. He might, though, have committed a civil offence. So what is the difference between civil and criminal offences?

In a criminal case someone (called the defendant) is prosecuted – usually by the police – for behaviour which is harmful to society. It may at the same time be harmful to another individual, but the main aim of the criminal law is not to avenge that person's sense of injury but to punish a person found guilty. In a civil case, however, one person sues another for some wrong they have done him or her. The same behaviour can in fact break both the civil and the criminal law, and such instances serve to point up the differences between them. For example, suppose Jackie is crossing the road when from nowhere Dave – who is drunk – knocks her down and injures her. Dave is then prosecuted by the police for drinking and driving. He is found guilty. The penalty is a fine and the loss of his licence. That is of no use to Jackie, though, who is off work for four weeks because of the injury. So she sues Dave for compensation for the injury to cover what she has lost: loss of earnings, damaged clothes, plus a sum for 'pain and suffering'.

In each case both the question to be decided by the court and the penalty are different. So is the standard of proof. In the criminal case the standard of proof is higher and a jury has to be 'satisfied so that they are sure' that Dave was guilty of drinking and driving, whereas in the civil case, the court only needs to be sure 'on the balance of probabilities' that it was Dave's fault that Jackie was hurt, and to assess just how hurt she was.

The Criminal Courts

The Old Bailey may have a certain glamour but 97 per cent of all criminal cases are dealt with in Magistrates' Courts, or District Courts in Scotland. In fact anyone who has committed a criminal offence (whether Jack the Ripper or Jack the Lad) has to go through a Magistrates' Court first.

Most cases are heard by a 'bench' of three 'lay' magistrates – also called Justices of the Peace, or JPs – who are not paid or legally qualified. They are chosen by the Lord Chancellor's Office from the local community. There are also about 55 paid magistrates – called 'Stipendiaries' because they receive a 'stipend', or salary – who are like mini-judges. They are legally experienced and sit in some of the busiest inner-city courts.

For a minor offence – a 'summary offence' – you get a summons to appear in the Magistrates' Court on a certain date. For a more serious offence you will first be charged by the police. If they release you on bail, you will be told when to appear in court, but if kept in detention, you will normally be brought before a court within 24 hours.

Summary offences can only be dealt with by magistrates, but serious offences – 'indictable offences' – are referred by magistrates to trial by jury at a higher criminal court, the Crown Court, or the Sheriff Court in Scotland. At a Magistrates' Court the magistrate hears the evidence, decides whether you are guilty, and passes sentence, but at a Crown Court a jury listens and decides whether you are guilty (the verdict), and, if you are, a judge decides how to deal with you (the sentence).

In between summary and indictable offences is another category – 'offence triable either way', for which you can choose whether to be tried in the Magistrates' Court or the Crown Court.

The maximum sentence that magistrates can impose is six months (or a maximum of 12 months for two or more offences together). If after trial in the Magistrates' Court the magistrate thinks that six months is not long enough, he can commit you to

YOU ARE HERE
TO BE TRIED
BEFORE A JURY
OF YOUR
PEERS.

J. J. G.

a Crown Court for sentence. If you disagree with the verdict or sentencing of the Crown Court or Sheriff Court you have the right of appeal to higher courts (see p. 140).

Apart from trials and sentencing, magistrates can also grant bail, keep you in detention to await trial, hear evidence to see if you should be committed to the Crown Court for trial, and order a probation officer report. They also deal with some family disputes.

Juvenile Courts

If you are under 17 and charged with a criminal offence you are most likely to appear before a Juvenile Court. As in the Magistrates' Court, you come before a 'lay bench' of three magistrates, but ones who are specially chosen for their experience in dealing with young people.

Unlike that of adult courts, where the main point is to punish you if you have broken the law, the aim of the Juvenile Court is to help you not to offend again. For this reason, hearings are in private and only people connected with the case are allowed to be present. If the case is found proved against you, the ways of dealing with you are different from sentences in the adult courts.

The Civil Courts

Most civil cases are heard in County Courts in England, Wales and Northern Ireland, and in Sheriff Courts in Scotland. The more serious ones go to the High Court or to the Court of Session in Scotland. You might want to take a car dealer to court, for example, if you found a car you bought from him had a serious defect and he refused to give you a refund. Or you could be taken to court yourself by your landlord for failing to pay the rent, in which case he might be asking the court not only for the arrears of the rent but also to evict you for non-payment.

To sue someone in the civil courts you have to be 18, unless your claim is for a debt. If you are under 18, you have to have an adult (called a 'next friend') to act for you. County Courts deal mostly with money claims up to £5,000, though under legislation proposed at the time of writing this is to be increased to £10,000.

The main civil cases County Courts cover are debt claims up to £5,000, landlord and tenant disputes, wills (if less than £30,000), bankruptcy, undefended divorce and domestic violence cases.

> **66**
>
> **A special procedure in the County Courts for 'small claims' aims to encourage you to bring a claim yourself without having to pay expensive legal costs.**
>
> **99**

Small claims

There is a special procedure in the County Courts for claims of £500 or less – 'small claims' – which aims to encourage you to bring a claim yourself without having to pay expensive legal costs (the £500 limit has stood for a long time and may well be increased). In Scotland, where the cases are held in Sheriff Courts, the limit is £750. For this purpose, the normal rule that you have to pay the legal costs of the other side if you lose (apart from your own of course) does not apply, and for this reason, this sort of case is often known as a do-it-yourself or DIY claim.

A typical sort of DIY claim is a claim for money back paid for faulty goods (eg a sewing machine or a pair of shoes), a claim for compensation for faulty workmanship (this could be a laundry failing to remove a stain on dry cleaning or a garage not repairing a car properly), non-payment of a debt, or a claim for compensation for damage to your car after an accident.

To make a small claim, write to the offending person (the defendant) first, sending the letter by recorded delivery, setting out the basis of your claim and giving him or her seven days to pay or to come up with satisfactory proposals for settling your claim. If the response is inadequate or non-existent, get the necessary forms from your nearest County Court or Sheriff Court and complete them. Most County Courts have standard forms for the all-important Particulars of Claim which set out the details of your case. You will need to complete one Request Form, two copies of the Particulars of Claim and pay the relevant Court Fee (which is recoverable if you win) and then either take them or send them to the court. It is best to take them if you can as the court staff will help you if you have made a mistake or missed out something.

The court will then issue a summons which it will send to the defendant. If he or she fails to pay up or admit your claim, there will be a preliminary hearing – called a pre-trial review – which is to help you and the defendant make the necessary preparations for the full hearing. Sometimes the case is settled at this stage, but if not, a date will then be fixed for the hearing. You will need to prepare for the hearing – or trial – by bringing together all the documents you need in support of your claim and making sure that any witnesses you have can come to the hearing – and know what to say!

At the hearing itself, you and your witnesses give your evidence first and the defendant can cross-examine your wit-nesses. He or she then gives his or her side of the story, and you equally have the right to cross-examine the defendant and his or her witnesses. Then you both have to sum up the case, and the Registrar – the County Court official who deals with small claims – will give judgement.

Even if you win, that may not be the end of the story. If the defendant fails to pay, you may have to 'enforce' the judgement to get your money. This could be by sending in the bailiffs to confiscate goods to the necessary value, by making the defendant bankrupt, or by getting an order for instalments to be paid out of his or her earnings. Sometimes you can even get an order that the defendant's bank pays you what is owed out of his or her bank account.

Large claims

For complex and expensive claims you do not go to a County Court at all, but to the High Court, or Court of Session in Scotland. The High Court consists of three main divisions: the Queen's Bench Division, the Family Division and the Chancery Division. The Queen's Bench Division is the main court for disputes over £5,000. It also has a Divisional Court where judges can review decisions made by tribunals, government departments or similar authorities who have misused their powers and thereby affected the rights of an individual or group. The Family Division deals with defended divorces, adoption, wardship and other disputes relating to people under 18. The Chancery Division deals with probably the most complicated areas of law: tax, interpretation of wills, company matters, trusts, property settlements. Chancery judges are supposed to be the cleverest judges, and if you read in the paper that Judge X has left in his will £100,000 gross, 'nil net', in other words that he has arranged his estate so there is no tax to pay on it, you can be sure he was a Chancery Judge.

In Scotland the Court of Sessions is divided into the Inner House and the Outer House. Generally the Inner House acts as a court of appeal, and the Outer hears new cases.

The Appeal Courts

A person who wishes to appeal against a court's decision can apply for the case, whether civil or criminal, to go to the Court of Appeal, or to the Court of Session in Scotland for civil cases and the High Court of Justiciary for criminal ones. The Court of Appeal has a civil division presided over by the Master of the Rolls, at present Lord Donaldson, and a criminal division presided over by the Lord Chief Justice, at present Lord Lane. From there it is sometimes possible to appeal to the House of Lords if the case involves a point of particular importance. But only about one in 40 cases goes from the Court of Appeal to the House of Lords. Such cases are not heard by the whole House, but by the highest judges in the land who also sit in the House of Lords. Unlike other judges in the higher courts, the Law Lords do not wear wigs or gowns but simply dark suits. Under Scottish Law some civil cases can go on appeal to the House of Lords, but no criminal ones, the High Court of Justiciary being the last court of appeal.

The EC (The Common Market)

Outside the British courts is one whose decisions even the highest English and Scottish courts must follow: the European Court of Justice. It decides on conflicts between the law of individual states who are members of the European Community and EC law, and is mainly concerned with economic matters.

There is also the European Court of Human Rights in Strasbourg, which decides on human rights issues like prisoners' rights, corporal punishment, rights of immigrants and mental patients. Individuals can take their cases to it if they do not get satisfaction in the courts of their own country, or if they consider their own laws unjust. However, the European Convention on Human Rights is not recognised by our courts and so cannot be enforced in them.

Tribunals

In addition to the courts there are about 60 different kinds of tribunals. They are much like civil courts but deal with special areas of the law mostly to do with the welfare state.

Industrial tribunals deal with disputes between employer and employee. If you are dismissed from your job unfairly then you may be able to go to the industrial tribunal – depending on your length of service – and apply for compensation or even for your job back.

Social security appeal tribunals handle appeals against decisions by the DSS or the Department of Employment affecting state benefits. If, for instance, you lose your job and apply for unemployment benefit, you may find you are disqualified from receiving it for the first six weeks. If the dismissal was through no fault of your own, such as because of redundancy, you can then appeal to the tribunal.

Immigration tribunals deal with appeals against Home Office decisions about immigration control. Let us say you are an overseas student, and you have been refused an extension of stay because you are living in a council flat and the Home Office say you are spongeing off the state. You can appeal against this decision to an immigration adjudicator.

There is no legal aid (see p.146) for most tribunals and the hearings are supposed to be informal and cheap. Although you can handle it all yourself, it is normally advisable to have someone represent you, such as a person from one of your free local advice centres or Law Centre. There are time limits for taking cases to tribunals – three months in the case of an unfair dismissal claim.

Witnesses

You do not have to appear as a witness in either a criminal or a civil case unless you receive a witness summons (called a subpoena). If you fail to turn up in court after receiving a subpoena, you can be fined or even sent to prison for contempt of court.

Sentencing

If you are found guilty of a crime, there are various ways the state can punish you. There are four main aims in sentencing – punishment, prevention, deterrence and reform. The kind of sentence given depends not only on the nature of the offence but also on previous convictions and the age and background of the offender.

The main types of sentence are imprisonment, probation, disqualification (for motoring offences), bind over, fine or compensation order, and absolute or conditional discharge, which is a conviction without punishment. In the case of conditional discharge, if you get into trouble again in the period set by the court, you can then be punished for the original offence.

In the case of a bind over you have to be of good behaviour for a set period of up to a year or else pay a specific sum of money. This is usually in the region of £50–£100 if you are under 17.

Probation is not applicable if you are under 17; it means being placed under the supervision of a probation officer, normally for one or two years.

If you are under 21 you are not sent to jail but are sentenced to 'youth custody'. This is normally for four months or over, and cannot exceed 12 months for those under 17. There is no borstal any more. The court can also postpone sentencing for up to six months, whatever your age, taking into account how you behaved during that time (called deferred sentence). If you are over 21 it can also suspend sentence, which means that you do not serve the sentence unless you commit another offence within a specified time.

There are other special types of sentence for people under 21, the main aim of which is to reform:

1 The police can just administer an instant caution if you admit to an offence and your parent or guardian agrees. However as it goes on the record, you should never agree to a caution if you have done nothing wrong.

2 You can be placed under a supervision order, which means you are supervised by a person – usually a social worker or probation officer – whose job is to 'advise, assist and befriend' you.

3 You can be given a Supervised Activity order, which means taking part in organised activity for up to 30 days a year. It could be community work or evening classes or you could be ordered to stay at home at night, or not go to football matches, for example. Or you may have an Attendance Centre Order, according to which you have to take part in organised activities – or something like a course in your spare time – at a centre run by the police.

4 If you are 16, you can do community service for between 40 and 120 hours.

5 If you are male and under 20, you can be sent to a detention centre for between 21 days and four months. The idea is to give you a – 'short, sharp, shock', through a rigorous physical regime.

You should never agree to a caution if you have done nothing wrong.

After a specific period of time, most ex-criminals are given a chance to 'wipe the slate clean'. A conviction becomes 'spent', which means that you have the legal right to say that you don't have a previous conviction. The terms are set out in the 1974 Rehabilitation of Offenders Act. For example, the period for a fine to be set aside is five years, or for a disqualification, the length of the disqualification. However, you can never be 'rehabilitated' if you go to prison for longer than 2½ years. You also have to reveal a conviction when applying for certain jobs, such as social worker or youth worker.

Victims of crime

If you have suffered from the criminal act of someone else, you should report it to the police as soon as possible. This is not just to enable them to find the criminal, because in order to get compensation – for example, insurance after a burglary – it is almost always necessary to show that you have reported the crime to the police. Everybody is familiar with the 999 number to use in an emergency, but if you are reporting a crime that has already happened, such as finding your flat has been burgled, or otherwise wish to contact the police, look up the number of your local police station in the telephone directory, under 'Police'. Advice on measures to avoid burglary is free from police stations.

In certain situations you may not feel like reporting the crime to the police straight away, even if you feel that you should. Rape is a common example, in which case you can contact the Rape Crisis Centre (see p.242). There may also be a local victim support scheme in your area where you can seek help and advice – contact your Citizens Advice Bureau for the address.

There are a number of ways in which victims of crime can recover compensation. The main ones are through the Criminal Injuries Compensation Board, if you are injured as a result of a violent crime or in trying to prevent a crime; through the Motor Insurers Bureau, if you have been injured in a road accident and the driver was not insured or cannot be traced; or, where property is involved, by getting a compensation or restitution order from a court. Consider also claiming insurance where possible or even taking the criminal to court in a civil action (the Yorkshire Ripper is an extreme example of someone who was taken to court for compensation, by the mother of one of his victims).

Where to get help

Knowing your rights is one thing, but knowing where to get the right kind of advice and legal help can be even more important.

For general help of all kinds your local Citizens Advice Bureau (CAB) is usually the best starting point. You may have an independent advice agency in your area you can go to. CABs are free, you do not usually have to make an appointment, and they may be able to help you sort out your problem there and then. If not, they should know where to go for the best source of help.

If it is legal advice or representation you need, the CAB – or advice agency – will direct you to a free legal advice session or Law Centre if you have one locally, or to a solicitor.

Law Centres specialise mainly in areas of the law for which you cannot get legal aid (see below), such as housing, employment, social security and immigration. They are run by the community for the community and so operate within a defined geographical area. Even though they specialise, most Law Centres run free legal advice sessions on general legal problems during the day or in the evening.

For most criminal cases, or cases involving accidents, injury or family problems, you will need to see a solicitor. You may qualify for legal aid, so do not be put off by the idea that it might cost a lot, or that it will be a frightening experience. True, some solicitors do charge a fortune, some are very stuffy and others are just bad, but this is not always the case. Your local advice centre should be able to point you in the direction of the best one for your problems, or a friend or member of your family may know of a good one. If you want to check for yourself, you can get hold of something called the 'Solicitors Referral List' from your local library or advice centre. This has the names of individual solicitors in each solicitors' office with details of what they specialise in. The list will also show you which solicitors give a 'fixed fee interview', that is, half an hour for £5, but few solicitors take part in the scheme as they do not consider it worth it for the fee received.

Legal aid

If you cannot afford to pay yourself, then the State may pay all or part of your solicitor's charges. You can get initial advice and legal help on the 'Green Form Scheme' (so-called because the form is green) or Pink Form in Scotland. This covers things like writing letters, negotiating on the phone, attending police stations, or getting medical reports. It allows solicitors to do work up to the value of £50 (roughly two hours altogether). However, in some cases solicitors can apply to the Law Society (the solicitors' professional body) to do extra work.

Anyone who is 16 or over can get this form of help as long as they do not have too much money. For a single person, this means roughly under £100 per week net income and under £800 savings. If your income is more than £60 per week net, you may have to pay a contribution to the solicitor's charge. If you are on income support, you automatically qualify for free assistance. You can still get it if you are under 16, but an adult normally has to sign the form for you.

For going to court, both in civil and criminal cases, you can get legal aid to cover your solicitor's charges and any court costs. In civil cases, if you are under 18, you have to have an adult – often a parent – actually to instruct the solicitor, to apply for legal aid and bring the case for you, except if suing over a debt. The main sorts of civil cases for which legal aid is available are divorce and personal injury. The Law Society (or in Scottish law the Law Society of Scotland) decides whether you are eligible or not, taking into account whether you have a reasonable case.

In criminal cases, you do not need an adult to instruct a solicitor for you if under 18. You apply direct to the Magistrates' Court (District Court in Scotland) by filling out two forms, one with your reasons for needing legal aid and the other with details of your means. It is then up to the Magistrates' Court whether to grant you legal aid or not.

Jury service

Even if you are conscientiously law-abiding, and always avoid disputes, you are still more than likely to end up in court at some time in your life. Once you are over 18 you are eligible for jury service. Selection is done on a random basis, so you can be called at any time, and indeed may be called more than once.

You can only be excused if there is a particularly 'good reason', such as having to do exams or looking after a close relative. Going on holiday is not considered to be a sufficiently good reason. If you believe that you should be excused, you write to the Summoning Officer, explaining why. If you fail to comply with a jury summons you can be fined up to £400. If your boss refuses to let you have time off work he or she could be prosecuted for contempt of court.

L IVING AT HOME

If you're 18 or more when you leave school, you've got the option of leaving home and setting up house somewhere else. You can leave home when you're 16 if you've got your parents' consent, but for a variety of reasons, most school-leavers remain at home with their parents or guardians for some time after they've left.

Leaving home is a big step at a time when there are lots of other new experiences to sort out as well, so many school-leavers who stay haven't made a conscious decision to do so. Going away to college can be a useful half-way house between staying in the parental home and becoming completely independent, but if you've got a job within easy reach of home, or you're going to a local college or joining a training scheme, you may well find that staying at home is both desirable and essential. Most people find that a combination of lack of money and the need for security means that the decision to move out is put off for a while.

If your relationship with your parents hasn't been too good, it could improve when you leave school – after all you're now having to face many of the same pressures that they do, whatever the family background. And if you get on well with them, living at home has all sorts of advantages. It's cheaper, the surroundings are often more cheerful than many rented places, and loneliness shouldn't be a problem.

It's easy to feel frustrated and trapped if your relationships with some or all the other members of the family are already strained and you know you've got to stay at home. Families can fall out for good if tensions are allowed to build up and boil over. But if the situation feels bad to you, remember that it's probably as bad for everyone else in the house. Sorting out a few basic living arrangements in the beginning should help to avoid some potentially nasty flare-ups later on.

What to contribute

Whatever your relationship with your parents, one of the first things you should settle with them is what you're going to contribute to the household kitty. Not many families can afford to support an extra adult for nothing, but many people don't like the idea of asking for money from their sons and daughters – even though they are now adults. It's worth broaching the subject before they do, and try and insist they take something, even if it's just to give them a bit extra to spend on themselves.

> **If the situation feels bad to you, remember that it's probably as bad for everyone else in the house.**

For some idea of actual amounts, have a look at the cost of rent or mortgage that your parents are paying, the rates, gas, electricity, water rates and telephone, and how much is spent on shopping each week, then work out your share of the total as an adult in the house. After this, work out how much you think you can afford (look at the suggestions on budgeting in the 'Money Matters' chapter) – you may well find that the two sums don't match! Make your parents an offer. Even if it's only a few quid a week it will help to raise your status in the household from dependent to equal – morally, if not in practice!

There may be a period when your parents or guardians are going to have to keep you for nothing anyway, especially if you're waiting to go to college, waiting to claim benefit or can't start your job for a few weeks. There are no national guidelines on pocket money – that's something you'll have to work out between you, but if you don't want or don't like to take a handout, suggest a loan that you'll pay back when you start earning or can claim benefit.

If you are receiving social security, one indication of what to contribute is to look at the amount of personal allowance single people living away from home are left with after paying their board. Ask at the local DSS office what current amounts are, and use this as a baseline. Your own situation will also depend on parental income, the number of other people in the house and how much it costs to run the home. But if money is a source of contention and disagreement, the DSS guidelines are worth sticking to: show them to your parents so they can see there's official backing to your calculations.

It isn't usually possible to get extra money towards household expenses if you're on social security, even if your parents give you a rent book to establish you as a tenant within their home (see p.156). You have to prove you run a completely separate household, with separate commitments, separate sleeping accommodation and so on. Under present DSS and housing benefit rules you are nearly always considered a 'non-householder' when living with relatives, except in special circumstances. Still, it's worth checking out at the DSS if you fall into the special categories, as they are there to help you.

Getting on with each other

It is not just living with your family that can cause friction. Sharing with people of your own age can have its problems (see p.169)! However, as you've probably been living at home for years, if they are there the tensions have unfortunately had a long time to build up on both sides. Even if your relationships are good, make sure everyone knows where they are with regard to household chores, cooking, shopping and especially social life. It's often difficult for the family to accept that once you've left school you want to be treated as the independent adult you now are, especially if you've got a job and can contribute financially. Conversely, being unemployed, and

"I keep telling him he can't really like it here."

therefore around the house a lot, can cause friction. As with all these basically human problems, the best thing is to try and talk about them. Ask the rest of the family what they expect from you, and let them know how you would like to be treated. You might be surprised to learn that they weren't even aware of some of the things you bring up, and you could be surprised by their side of things too. You may think housework is boring, but someone's got to do it, and your parents probably hate it too. You'd have to do it all yourself if you lived away from home, so in a way it's unfair to expect parents to continue to do everything for you if you're living with them *and* ask them to treat you as an equal. It's easy to think, 'Well, if I was living alone I'd be able to do A, B and C', but you'd also have to do 'X, Y and Z' which may not be so pleasant. So while you are in your parents' home you've got to respect some of the rules and regulations they choose to run it by. After all they may have been looking forward to having some time to themselves when their children left home and if financial constraints don't make this possible, your parents may feel frustrated and disappointed as well.

If things really get bad and you can't communicate with your parents, see if there is a mutual friend or relative who can act as a go-between to clear the air.

Privacy is often at the root of dissension within a family of adults; theirs as well as yours. If you've got your own bedroom, turn it into your own private living area and ask others in the household to respect it. You could even make separate eating arrangements if it's feasible, buying and cooking your own food, if it doesn't offend everyone else.

It's virtually impossible to cover all the problems you are likely to come across if you continue to live at home once you've left school; each situation will have its own specific dilemmas, but the best advice is to always try and share your feelings and problems with somebody else. There is a multitude of national and local organisations set up to deal with the whole area of housing, but they usually concern themselves with issues like finding and keeping accommodation, the legal aspects of renting and so on; few have facilities for dealing with the more psychological aspects of living at home. However, CHAR (the Campaign for the Single Homeless), Shelter (a housing charity and pressure group), and the National Youth Bureau will offer advice and have published a number of publications that are well worth a look. (See p. 242 for addresses.)

Never forget, you are not alone; there are millions of other young people experiencing exactly the same frustrations as you. Seek them out in your area, at clubs, community centres, churches or other youth groups. Talk to the workers there as well, they will have dealt with lots of similar situations, and will be able to suggest ways of dealing with them. If things do get desperate don't hesitate to ring the Samaritans; they won't preach to you and can offer sound practical advice.

And finally a word about you and the rest of the world (or your street at least!) now that school's behind you and fading fast. *You* may be able to afford and enjoy a whole new social life, with money for records and late nights out, but the rest of the family and the neighbours might not be so eager to share it with you, so spare them a thought when you play music or come in late.

MOVING AWAY

Before you slam the door of your parents' home in anger for the last time – or even if you're going with their blessing – think about what you're taking on. It is one of the biggest decisions you will have made in your life so far. Finding a place to live is tough – and it's getting harder all the time. In recent years the number of young people sleeping on the streets of large cities like London has swollen dramatically, and what you are leaving behind has to be spectacularly awful to face joining them as an alternative. Even when you've found somewhere which you can afford and which is warm and dry, there are still a lot of practical problems to face and responsibilities to take on – paying the rent and other bills such as gas and electricity, dealing with your landlord, finding people to live with, sometimes furnishing and decorating, cleaning, cooking and so on.

> **Prepare yourself by getting references for possible use with landlords and save up for the deposit.**

Of course, you may have no choice in the matter, either because you're going to college in another town, or your parents have thrown you out, or because life has become too intolerable at home or simply because you haven't got any parents or a home. But if you do have a choice in the matter, spend an extra day or so thinking about it one last time and try checking out some of the options suggested below first, while you've still got a home to go back to after a heavy day's flat-hunting. Finding a place to live takes *time* and you'll have to face some disappointments before you're finally settled. Best of all, prepare yourself by getting references for possible use with landlords and save up for the deposit you'll almost undoubtedly need.

If you've got nowhere to go *tonight* – or you're about to be evicted – and you've got no friends or relatives who'll take you in, don't panic. There's probably a hostel or other night shelter in your town that will take you in while you sort things out, even if you've got no money. It won't be wonderful but it'll give you a breathing space (see p. 163 for more details). Alternatively, you could stay in a bed and breakfast hotel but you will have to pay out of your own pocket until you get housing benefit (see p.166) from the DSS, which could take a few weeks.

There are two main sources of rented accommodation – the council and private landlords. There are also housing associations and co-ops, and for the better-off, homes to buy. If you're desperate, there's temporary squatting and short-life property. In this section we look at all these options – your best chance is to try as many as possible, as well as asking all your friends and relatives if they know of a place going – much housing changes hands through word of mouth.

A word of warning. The rules outlined in this section apply to England and Wales; sometimes different rules apply in Scotland and Northern Ireland, so if you live in either of these check with a local advice centre before proceeding.

Renting from a private landlord

Nearly all private rented flats are furnished which makes them more expensive, as part of your rent goes towards paying for the furniture, however horrible it is. Unfurnished flats normally only change hands on payment of a large fee for 'fixtures and fittings', which in fact is just a way of selling the tenancy, and in any case unfurnished flats are very hard to find.

There is no longer any legal distinction between unfurnished and furnished lettings. In much privately rented accommodation, the landlord lives on the premises, however. The law relating to how long you can stay in this sort of place is different since the landlord is able to get you out more easily (see below).

Finding a house, flat or room

Apart from word of mouth, which is probably the most common way of getting somewhere to rent, there are three main ways of finding this type of accommodation: adverts in shop windows, adverts in local papers and accommodation agencies or estate agents. Although not many places are advertised in shop windows, it is often a good way of finding somewhere in the area you want. It's simply a matter of 'getting on your bike' and traipsing round all the local shops. There's one big advantage, too – it's free. Very often shop window or local paper adverts are from people who already have a flat, but need someone else to share it with them. And while you're out checking on shops, drop into any local colleges. They have notice-boards which often advertise accommodation and, even better, sometimes produce lists of possible places which are hung up on the boards. It doesn't matter that you're not a student.

To have any chance of finding a place through adverts in the local papers, you have to be quick off the mark. Buy the paper as soon as it comes out – from the newspaper office if possible, as weekly papers can often be obtained on the evening before publication and dailies will be hot off the press – and get phoning straight away. Be ready to go round immediately to the place to view it.

One of the easiest ways of finding somewhere to live is to share a flat – people often advertise for 'flat-shares' in newspapers and magazines. But if you do share with people you don't know, make sure you meet them first and decide if you think you will all get on under one roof (see p. 167). In any event, they will probably want to meet you first, possibly seeing several people and selecting the one they like best.

Accommodation agencies, particularly in London, can be a rip-off. Many of them will try to charge you before finding you somewhere, which is illegal. Don't give them any money unless they have actually found you somewhere – and you have already agreed with the landlord to take it. If the agency is successful in finding you a place you will normally have to pay a couple of weeks' rent to them as an agency fee. Estate agents tend to be more honest but rarely have anything at the cheaper end of the market. However, they're worth a try if several of you are planning to share as they sometimes have whole houses to let.

One thing to bear in mind about finding a privately rented place is that you need a lot of cash immediately. Most landlords will ask for one to four weeks' rent in advance and a similar amount as a deposit against any damage you may cause. And you may have had to pay an accommodation agency as well. If you are on income support, you may be able to borrow the money from the Department of Social Security (DSS) for the deposit and the advance rent but you will have to fight very hard for it, and it is likely they will point you in the direction of some other source of loans.

Make sure that the landlord gives you a rent book and a receipt for every payment, including your deposits. It is a crime for landlords to refuse to give their tenants a rent book, and you should tell your local Rent Officer immediately (look the telephone number up in the telephone directory under 'Rent').

If the place is furnished there should be an inventory of the contents.

Make sure you know exactly what your responsibilities are with regard to repairs etc. If the place is furnished there should be an inventory of the contents – if the landlord doesn't offer one (most do) it's worth making one yourself and getting the landlord to agree it so that you can't be charged when you leave for removing or damaging items which weren't there in the first place. Make sure you keep a copy of the inventory in a safe place. On the other hand, if you break a window by mistake don't expect the landlord to come round and mend it for you – at least without charging you. Equally, the landlord is usually responsible for the maintenance of the exterior (find out before you move in!), so if the roof leaks let him know. If he won't do anything about it, go and get advice from a Citizens Advice Bureau (CAB) or a Law Centre.

All these things should be covered in a tenancy agreement between you and the landlord, setting out both parties' rights and duties. However, because accommodation is so short, you may well not be offered one and the landlord may avoid negotiating one. If you do get one it is likely to have lots of conditions, such as not allowing you to keep a pet, which you may not like but which you'll have to accept to get the flat. At least read it first to ensure that it's not too outrageous. The law actually protects you from signing all your rights away so in practice the agreement may be meaningless anyway.

Rent assessment committees

For many lettings, it is possible to have your rent examined by the local rent assessment committee. To apply, find out from the council or the phone book where the committee is situated and get the relevant form to fill in. The job of the committee is to determine what they think the rent should be. They make their decision entirely on what they consider the market value to be, looking at such things as the value of similar properties in the area. What you can afford or consider to be fair are not relevant. You can therefore find that you are told to pay more rent than before, so it is worth doing a lot of homework as to other rents charged for properties in the neighbourhood before you proceed.

Eviction

A disadvantage of renting privately is that in many cases you can get evicted quite easily. In theory, unless the landlord lives on the premises, you should be able to stay as long as you want. In practice, landlords use all sorts of fiddles to make sure they don't give you 'security of tenure' – which is legalspeak for being able to stay forever. These range from giving you 'breakfast', so that you qualify as a lodger, to making it a holiday let or a short-term let. Under the latter, he can let for six months and then evict you any time afterwards on giving two months' notice.

The law is very complicated and changes all the time as judges make rulings in particular cases, so seek legal advice from a Law Centre or CAB before moving out. In any case, you cannot be evicted without a court order. Just because you are sent a 'notice to quit' doesn't mean you have to leave immediately. The landlord still has to go to court to get a possession order and you have the right to go to the hearing to defend it.

Even if the landlord is trying to evict you, continue paying the rent, otherwise your failure to pay, for whatever reason, makes it much more likely that a judge will decide against you should the case get to court. Sometimes it is possible to withhold your rent to pay for repairs the landlord has failed to carry out. But don't try doing that without seeking legal advice as it's very complicated.

Lodgings

This used to be a very common form of accommodation for people moving away from home for the first time, particularly for students, but nowadays there are relatively few places. However, council tenants now have the right to take in lodgers so the numbers may increase again. Lodgings usually consist of a room in a family home and sometimes you may be provided with breakfast and possibly an evening meal. If you are a student, your college Accommodation Officer will have lists of approved lodgings (see p.81).

Living in someone else's home may not be what you want to do but it could be just what you need to make the break or if you're setting up in a different town. Legally, you have to negotiate the rent with the landlady or landlord, and you can be evicted quite easily as you're a licensee rather than a tenant.

The council

Your local council will have a housing department. Even if you think you will not be a priority for them, it is worth going along to see them and asking about your chances of getting a council home.

There is a shortage of council housing almost everywhere so at first you will have to go on a waiting list. People under 18 cannot legally be tenants (see p.168) and therefore the council will not accept them on the list. Otherwise you have a right to sign on to it, even if the council says that you don't qualify because you don't have any children or they have a higher age limit of, say, 25.

Although there is a law called the Housing (Homeless Persons) Act which obliges the council to find homes for people, it only applies to very specific 'priority need' categories – essentially families with children still in full-time education, pensioners, pregnant women, people with disabilities or who are ill and those considered 'vulnerable'. You may have a chance of fitting into the last category if you are very young and the council thinks you could be taken advantage of sexually or financially. Otherwise, if you don't fit into any of those groups, the council is merely obliged to provide you with 'advice and assistance'. That can mean anything from just handing you a list of local bed and breakfast hotels to phoning around all possible local sources of housing.

In most areas, the waiting list is just that – you wait and wait and wait. Single people have less priority than families and you will be competing with pensioners – who also have a higher priority – for the small number of bedsits or one bedroom flats. Allocation of council housing is usually done according to a points system; you get points for living in overcrowded conditions, if you're in poor health, if you've got children and so on. Ask the council officials to explain what the local system is and how many points you need to qualify for housing and how long they think you will have to wait.

Special schemes

A few councils, particularly in the larger towns, have special schemes for young people which are run outside the points system. The most common are for 'hard to let' flats which families don't want to live in, usually because they are on estates with a bad reputation. However, virtually all the 'shared singles' schemes aimed at young single people sharing that sprung up in the 1970s have now ended. There are also sometimes special schemes for sons and daughters of existing council tenants, and for students. Ask about all these and keep on asking. Once you are on the waiting list, you have to keep on going back to the council to check whether anything's likely to come up. Be persistent.

If a friend or relative has moved out of a council flat, the council will not normally allow you to take on their accommodation unless you were living there before and are related to them. However, they are now obliged by law to allow tenants to take in lodgers.

Short-life housing

In many large towns there is a lot of property that has been left derelict because the council or local housing associations cannot afford to do it up. The better councils hand these houses over temporarily to local housing groups who 'patch repair' them and then let them to their members. The houses are often in a very bad condition and usually the people who live in them – the licensees – are expected to help maintain them. But they are cheap – just a few quid a week to cover the groups' expenses – and they can be very nice houses. The accommodation normally involves sharing with other people and you'll have to find your own furniture. Most short-life groups are run on a co-operative basis which means you'll be expected to put in some work to help run the organisation. Ask your local council or CAB if there are any such groups in your area.

Although the idea is 'short life', some people have stayed in the same houses for 10 years while others have to move on after a few months, but in either case, you are always living under the shadow of immediate eviction.

If there isn't a short-life housing group in your area but there's lots of empty property, you may want to set up your own – contact the Empty Property Unit at Shelter, 88 Old Street, London EC1 (071-253 0202). Or alternatively, you may want to squat in them . . .

Squatting

Squatting is not a crime. With a few exceptions, if you can get into a place which no one else is using without doing any damage, then you can make it your home. (The exceptions are that you can't squat on embassy property, in someone else's home or in a council or housing association property that's already been allocated to a tenant.)

First choose a place that is not going to be used soon by someone else. For example, don't squat in brand new homes which are bound to be allocated or bought in the near future. The most successful places to squat are in flats or unpopular council estates or in houses where the owner has disappeared or died. Try to find out who owns the property from local people – although neighbours are often, but by no means always, hostile if they know your intentions – or by ringing up the local rates office pretending to be a buyer (they won't tell you who owns it but they may tell you if it's council or housing association property).

The next – and major – problem is getting in. It is vital to change the lock on the door as quickly as possible because once you have done that, you're in possession. You may get into trouble with the police if they arrive and think you've caused any damage or are carrying tools intended for burglary. But legally, they shouldn't (although they do sometimes) force their way in and evict you after you've changed the lock.

Obtaining a gas or electricity supply in a squat can be difficult. If there is already a supply, make sure you take a meter reading and write to the Board (look it up under Gas or Electricity in the phone book) before starting to use the gas or electricity, otherwise you risk being prosecuted for stealing it. Do not tell the Boards that you are squatting! If there is no supply and the services have been cut off in the street, the Boards are unlikely to connect you and, even if they do, they will charge you several hundred pounds. In any event, they are likely to ask you for a deposit.

Obviously, when you squat you don't have to pay rent but if you know the owner you can offer, and if he does accept any rent from you, it may be your lucky day as you could then become secure tenants.

Eviction from a squat

To evict you, the owner will normally go to court for a possession order. You should be given notice of the court hearing but there is very rarely any legal defence to the owner's claim for possession. That process takes several weeks or even months and in the meantime you stay in the property. When the possession order is granted, the landlord can send in the bailiffs and it is a crime to resist them.

It is also possible for the owner to evict you without going to court for a possession order if he goes round to your squat and gets in when there is no-one there. However, most landlords, especially councils and housing associations, don't attempt to do this, and if they do try when you're in, they're committing a criminal offence. So make sure there's someone in all the time for a while after you move in until you know how the owner is going to react.

The Advisory Service for Squatters, 2 St Pauls Road, London N1 (071–359 8814, 2 pm to 6 pm) produces an excellent comprehensive and inexpensive guide, *The Squatter's Handbook*, which you should read before you squat. ASS also has up-to-date information on squatting groups and gives detailed advice on how to squat successfully.

Housing associations and co-ops

Housing associations are like mini councils, providing rented accommodation. They are run by management committees made up of local worthies and are given money by the government to build housing for rent to those most in need. Therefore, again, you're likely to be at the bottom of their list of priorities. Some have waiting lists, however, and, more importantly, some specialise in providing housing for young people. The council housing department or local CAB should have a list of associations which operate in your area.

Housing co-ops are a type of housing association run co-operatively by the tenants. They are usually small and have few vacancies, but it's worth asking if there are any local ones, and then seeing if you can join. The National Federation of Housing Associations (address on p.242) will be able to supply you with further information and with details of housing associations in your area.

Buying a place

Read no further if you don't have a job and some savings or very good references tucked away. Ironically, buying your home is the cheapest option in the long run but the initial cost is prohibitive for most young people. You can borrow the purchase price from a building society or bank – this is known as a mortgage. They won't usually lend you the full amount – 90 per cent is common, so you need savings for the rest, and you also need quite a lot of money for the legal and surveying fees, furniture and fittings, repairs and moving expenses. The amount of savings you need obviously varies but only about half of first-time buyers have £1,000 or less saved towards their home. Some builders and, on pressing, some building societies, do offer 100 per cent mortgages but only to people with a record of having paid rent regularly.

Buying your home is the cheapest option in the long run.

You don't have to be a married couple to get a mortgage: building societies are quite happy to lend to two or more friends sharing these days, as well as gay or unmarried couples. But, again, they will want to have proof of your ability to pay. They prefer to lend to people who have saved with them but will consider you if you haven't, especially at times when they're awash with cash. If you can't get a mortgage from a building society, try your local council. Although nowadays many of them no longer have money available for mortgages, some do have schemes that enable you to get preferential treatment from a society. Banks operate pretty much the same rules as the societies.

Building societies will lend between 2.5 and 3 times a person's annual income – that is, if you earn £9,000, they'll lend between £22,500 and £27,000 depending on what society you go to and whether they think you've got an honest face. If there's two of you, they'll lend a further amount equivalent to the second person's annual income.

Apart from the freedom of owning your own home, you also get enormous help in paying off the mortgage through tax relief which effectively means you get a quarter off the interest repayments (see p. 100). But owning your own home is a big responsibility as you have to pay for rates, gas, electricity and telephone, all repairs and maintenance. Also interest rates go up and down, affecting how much you have to pay each month.

At present, councils are encouraged to sell some of their properties. Various schemes operate; some involve selling to first-time buyers, others to existing tenants. Priority is usually given to people who live or work in the local authority area. Council homes are often sold at a price considerably lower than the market value and the council may well have a special mortgage facility as well. Call your local council housing department for details.

Hostels

These are the last resort. There are hostels or night shelters in most towns for homeless single people: some won't take in young people, whilst others are specifically aimed at them. The better hostels (like the YMCA) tend to have waiting lists. Many hostels provide some support for young people with social workers living on the premises or visiting regularly to act as a kind of halfway stage between living at home and completely on your own.

The hostels which take people in straight off the streets usually have a limit on the amount of time you can stay. They may, however, accept you for a night or two if you don't have any money whilst you sort things out with the DSS. Conditions in these hostels tend to be terrible. They often have huge dormitories and lots of very disturbed people, making it difficult to get a good night's sleep.

Most hostels are run by charities like the Salvation Army or by the local council. A few, called resettlement units, are run by the government and they can be even worse. They are supposed to help their residents 'resettle' into the community but in fact many people live in them for years.

Bed and breakfast hotels

Alternatively, you can go into a bed and breakfast hotel. This is a bit like getting lodgings (see p.158) except that you're in a hotel with lots of other people. Many hotels now specifically cater for unemployed single people who have nowhere to live.

B&B hotels can vary from proper hotels run by caring owners to shabby dumps where the breakfast is a packet of cornflakes and dried milk left once a week outside your room, but they are one way of getting a roof over your head quickly.

Until 1989 if you were in a B&B the DSS would pay your board and lodging up to a certain limit, but now you just receive housing benefit as you would if you lived somewhere else (see next page).

Special help

If you are a student, your college accommodation service may be able to find you somewhere to live. Many colleges have halls of residence specially for their students. Your college's National Union of Students office may also be able to help you (see p.81). Similarly, if you work for a large firm it may be able to provide housing.

A few councils operate 'key worker' schemes which give special priority to people doing vital jobs like nurses, teachers or bus drivers.

People on probation may also get special help from the probation office accommodation service. They usually have a close relationship with good local landlords and landladies.

Paying the rent

Housing is expensive. Even squatting costs money as you have to pay for repairs, furniture and bills for rates and services. You may, however, be able to obtain housing benefit if you are living in rented accommodation (see below).

IN CASE OF EMERGENCY BREAK GLASS AND USE.

"Mum gave it to me for Christmas – it's her front door key."

Council housing rents vary drastically from area to area and even between different estates. Although there's nothing you can do to get the rent reduced, you can take in lodgers to help pay it, or you may be eligible for housing benefit.

Housing benefit

If you are unemployed and on income support, you should get all your rent paid for under the housing benefit scheme. Although it is the local council which pays out the benefit, you have to go first to the DSS to sign on. If you are a private tenant or licensee, or a housing association or co-op tenant, your rent is sent to you. If you are a council tenant, you never see the money since the council simply pays it directly to itself, although you may still receive bills for heating and water charges. Even home-owners can receive housing benefit to pay their rates and they can also claim income support for the interest part of their mortgage repayments (see 'Unemployment' chapter).

If you're in full-time work and on low wages, or are getting another type of benefit, you may still be eligible to have part or all your rent paid for under the housing benefit scheme, but you cannot get help with the interest element of mortgage re-payments. It's worth applying anyway, so go along to the council's housing benefit section. The council assesses your needs according to your income and circumstances, such as whether you live on your own or have children or other dependants.

The housing benefit system is unbelievably complicated and many councils can't cope with their workload. Therefore, to get what you need, you may have to hassle the council and keep on at them until they pay up.

> **66**
>
> **The housing benefit system is unbelievably complicated and to get what you need, you may have to hassle the council and keep on at them.**
>
> **99**

Claimants moving into unfurnished accommodation may be able to get loans from the Social Fund to help with buying furniture (see 'Unemployment' chapter). However, these loans are discretionary, and you have to have been on income support for 26 weeks even to be considered. If you apply and are turned down, get advice or you could contact CHAR for help (the Campaign for the Single Homeless), 5–15 Cromer Street, London WC1 (071-833 2071).

Under 18s

If you're under 18 and you leave home without your parents' consent, it is unlikely that you will be forced to return, but care proceedings can be brought against you if you are thought to be in 'moral danger'.

There are extra problems for under-18-year-olds because you cannot have a tenancy in your own name and, of course, you can normally get income support. There are also very few hostels that will take in under 18s.

However, some councils will house you if you manage to persuade them that you have no alternative and that you are vulnerable. They can get round the fact that technically you can't be a tenant by granting you a tenancy that is 'held in trust' by the social services department or a responsible adult until you reach 18.

Living with other people

One big decision you face – although you may have no choice – is who you live with. Perhaps you already have a friend or two in mind or you intend to share with your boy or girlfriend. Either way, it's very important to discuss some groundrules before you move in over such things as bills, cooking, cleaning, lifestyle, responsibilities, shopping and much more.

There are a lot of basic points to think about. Do you all want to eat together and, in which case, who is going to do the cooking? Perhaps your friends may have outdated notions about women doing all the housework which would become difficult to cope with. Or will they want to stay up all night playing loud music when you have to get up early in the morning to go to work? And bills have to be paid on a fair basis so it's vital to discuss that before they come in (gas, electricity and phone bills all have to be paid every three months; and water rates are paid twice a year).

Cleaning, too, is a frequent source of dispute as some people don't mind living in a pigsty whilst others are meticulously tidy. Having lots of friends round, especially if they're noisy, may put other people off from having theirs round so that's something else to sort out. To avoid quarrels over money, it's best for everyone to contribute to a kitty for food (if you're all going to eat together) and for other household items.

Home at last

It's funny how many young people who set up on their own years ago still say they're 'going home' when they visit their parents. It takes a long time to feel really at home in a new place but there are lots of ways that you can make it feel 'lived in'. You can decorate it to your taste – with the landlord's permission, of course – you can invite friends round, get a telephone if you can afford it or even get a pet – though, again, you may need the landlord's permission and animals can take a lot of looking after.

If you're living on your own for the first time, life can be a bit lonely especially if you're in a new town. Try to get involved in local activities, perhaps by joining a community group, a political party (see 'Politics' chapter) or taking up evening classes which are much more interesting than school as the choice of subjects is vastly wider (see pp. 232–8 for lots of other suggestions). Some people find it easy to live on their own, whilst others can't cope with it at all. If you decide you can't, then quickly look for somewhere else to live. Don't try to sit it out and get depressed watching TV all the time.

Even if you did slam your parents' door in anger as you left, do keep in touch with them. You don't have to let them know where you are but they are almost bound to be worried about you, however badly you got on with them. The odd letter or phone call doesn't cost much, except possibly a bit of pride.

LOOKING AFTER YOURSELF

Health is something most people don't think about until they've lost it. There are things you can do to prevent ill health now and in the future and some of these are discussed later in this chapter. Up till now however you will probably have relied on your parents or guardians to organize things when there was something wrong with you, and you may want to continue this way for a while. But whether you have left school at that age or not, at 16 you reach the age of 'medical responsibility', which means that you don't have to have your parents' consent for any treatment available on the National Health Service. If you fall ill or suffer tooth ache or have an accident, especially if you've moved away from home, it is worth having some basic knowledge of the system and where to get treatment.

The National Health Service (NHS)

The National Health Service was set up in 1946 to provide comprehensive medical services free of charge to everyone who wishes to use them. It provides the whole range of health care, from family doctors to specialist hospital consultants, from child health clinics to opticians and dentists. The administration of such an immense organisation is extremely complex, and can sometimes be confusing to the user. The NHS is not a charity – every family in this country pays the equivalent of £22 per week in taxes to pay for it, and some of the services are no longer completely free, so it's your right to use it and to get the best possible service from it.

Your general practitioner (GP)

Most people's first contact with the NHS is through their family doctor or general practitioner (GP). Everyone should be registered with a GP. If you are already registered with your family's doctor there are many advantages in staying put. He or she will know your background and be aware of any particular medical problems, especially if you have been registered with the doctor since childhood. This is particularly important if you have special health needs (for example diabetes or epilepsy), or if you are disabled.

If you leave home to live on your own for the first time, it is especially important to find a doctor. Ask yourself a few questions about your preferences. For example, a male or female doctor? – younger or older? You should also look at the type of appointment system the doctor has – will you have to wait a long time to see him or her? – do surgery hours fit in with your work? – do you prefer an appointment system or 'drop in' system? One of the best ways to find a doctor to suit your needs is to ask a friend or neighbour to recommend one. Your local Community Health Council will also be able to give you advice on any of these matters, or you can ask at your local health centre.

> **66**
> **One of the best ways to find a doctor to suit your needs is to ask a friend or neighbour to recommend one.**
>

Community Health Councils (Local Health Councils in Scotland and District Committees in Northern Ireland) were set up to represent ordinary people in the NHS. You should find them listed in your local telephone directory under 'Community' or under the name of the individual Community Health Council – for example Liverpool Community Health Council is listed under 'L'.

If you have difficulty in getting on to a doctor's list, Family Practitioner Committees (FPCs) have a duty to find a doctor for you. (FPCs oversee the work of general practitioners in the various health districts.) FPCs are usually listed in the telephone books under 'Family'. In Scotland, this duty is undertaken by Health Boards (in the book under 'Health') and in Northern Ireland by the Central Services Agency, 27 Adelaide Street, Belfast BT2 8PH.

To register with a GP, telephone or call in to the surgery, and ask if there is room on the doctor's list. It's a good idea to take along your medical card which contains your NHS number, but don't worry if you don't have a card or have lost it – the doctor can request a copy from the Family Practitioner Committee. But once you have a medical card, keep it safely.

You can change your GP without having to give a reason. Find another GP who is willing to take you on, then ask your own GP to sign your medical card. Or you can write to the Family Practitioner Committee, Health Board or Central Services Agency, depending on where you live in the UK.

Consulting your GP

Your GP is normally the first port of call for any health worries, physical or mental symptoms. If necessary, she or he can then refer you to any of the other services within the NHS. As a general rule, any symptoms which persist are worth consulting your GP about. Always visit the doctor for persistent headaches, giddiness and tiredness, boils which don't heal, persistent coughs or hoarseness, a lump in your breast or elsewhere, persistent indigestion or difficulty in swallowing, persistent change in your normal bowel habits, or unexpected bleeding from any body opening. Use your common sense. Telephone the doctor's surgery for an appointment if that's the usual system, otherwise just turn up and join the queue. If you are feeling really bad most doctors will fit you in on the same day even if officially there aren't any spare appointments. But expect a longish wait in this case.

"Healthy bunch today, doctor: a footballer with bites, an aerobics dancer with a broken leg and a runover jogger."

Tell the doctor exactly what is wrong with you, or what you are worried about; there is no need to feel embarrassed. (Remember that your GP is a human being!) And if you don't understand his or her advice, say so, and persist until you are quite satisfied that you understand. In general your consent must be given to any examination and treatment; there are very few exceptions to this. (If you have continual problems in communicating with your GP, you might consider changing doctors – see above.)

If you are really too ill to go to the surgery and you need the doctor to visit you at home (a 'home visit'), let the surgery know as soon as possible. Most doctors' surgeries specify before 10 am. If you become ill outside of normal surgery hours your GP or a 'locum' (a stand-in doctor) may visit you at home. If you are too ill to go to work, don't forget to let your employer know in good time (see p.30).

If you are registered at a health centre or group practice, there is often a rota system in operation, so that when you call the doctor out, or need to make an appointment at the surgery at short notice, you may not always be seen by the same doctor.

It is also worth remembering that you don't have to wait until you're ill to visit your GP. She or he can provide you with contraceptive advice and services, maternity care, and preventive services such as smear tests and blood pressure checks. Some practices provide a special 'well-woman clinic' facility in addition to their normal services (see p. 180).

Confidentiality

In most cases, doctors can only pass on information when patients have given permission. For example, your doctor won't tell your parents anything without your permission, even if you're still living at home. Doctors may however pass on information required by other professionals involved in your treatment, or in certain special circumstances, such as when ordered to by a court of law.

Prescriptions

At present, most people have to pay a charge of £2.80 per item for prescriptions. There are certain exceptions to this: for example, there are no prescription charges for people on low incomes (which can include students) and for young people who are over 16 and under 19 and still at school or college. Ask at a post office or social security office for form AG1. This gives details of different groups entitled to free prescriptions, and an application form. If your doctor gives you a prescription take it to a dispensing chemist where a qualified pharmacist will make it up for you.

It is worth remembering that the pharmacist is a source of advice on a wide range of health matters. Many people take up valuable time with a doctor for minor illnesses which do not need treatment or can be helped by simple remedies that you can buy from your local chemist. Ask your pharmacist's advice on minor ailments, or any information you require on medicines, etc. He or she will tell you if you need to see a doctor.

Emergencies

In an emergency you can also go to a hospital casualty department (usually called an Accident and Emergency Unit). You should try to find out where the nearest Accident and Emergency Unit to your home is; not all hospitals have them. If you cannot get to the hospital under your own steam, dial 999 and ask for the ambulance service. This advice applies also if someone you're with has an accident or some other medical emergency, for instance if an older member of your family suffers a stroke or heart attack while you are there. Would you know what to do in these circumstances? If you are interested in learning first aid and resuscitation techniques, contact your local St John Ambulance or Red Cross branch.

Information, advice and complaints

Community Health Councils are sources of a wealth of information and advice relating to the NHS. They can advise you on finding a doctor or dentist, optician or chiropodist, or on family planning services in the area. They can provide detailed advice on your rights as a patient whether within the community or in hospital. They can also help with complaints.

Occasionally something may go wrong and it is your right to make a complaint and to get an explanation. Your CHC can advise you on how to make a complaint, whether it's about your GP or about treatment in hospital or other areas of the NHS. This is a very useful service, as complaints procedures can be quite complicated.

The National Consumer Council produces an excellent detailed guide called *Patients' Rights* which explains all you need to know about the NHS. Published by HMSO, the guide costs £1.50 from booksellers. However, your CHC or Citizens Advice Bureau should also be able to provide you with a free leaflet, 'Patients' Rights', which summarises the information contained in the book.

If you have to go to hospital

Going into hospital can be quite an unnerving experience, especially for the first time. If you have a condition that requires hospital treatment your GP will refer you to the Consultant and hospital best suited to the condition. Your GP should be able to answer any initial questions about it.

The first visit to hospital is usually as an 'outpatient', which means you are given an appointment during the day to a particular clinic, and you do not have to stay overnight. After assessment you may be put on a waiting list for 'inpatient' treatment, in other words, you will be asked to come in to one of the hospital wards and stay for a period of time. Don't be afraid to ask your GP or the hospital staff to explain anything you do not understand about your treatment or any other aspect of your stay in hospital.

Hospital doctors are doctors who have decided to specialise in a particular branch of medicine or surgery. They start their careers as House Officers (Junior Hospital Doctors) and progress to Senior House Officers, Registrars and Senior Registrars, some eventually becoming Consultants.

Care of patients in hospital rests largely with the nursing staff. There are also many other hospital staff on hand such as physiotherapists, radiographers, occupational therapists, and administrative staff. If you go to one of the large teaching hospitals there may well be student nurses and medical students. You may be asked if medical students can examine you, but you do not have to agree to this.

Inpatient treatment is completely free; you will only need pocket money for incidental expenses like soft drinks, newspapers and magazines. However, as an outpatient you do have to pay for prescriptions at the hospital pharmacy, unless you are in one of the exempted groups (see p.175).

Many hospitals give out patients' information booklets on admission to hospital. If you are given a booklet, read it thoroughly as it will contain a lot of useful information.

Benefits in hospital

If you have to go into hospital, any benefits you are receiving may be affected (see p.44). It is important to tell the DSS when you go into hospital, and also when you come out. If you are receiving income support, this may be immediately affected. After a stay of four weeks, attendance allowance and invalid care allowance stops. After eight weeks, sickness or invalidity benefit are reduced. But you may be able to claim fares or petrol for the journeys to and from hospital. For further information ask at your local Citizens Advice Bureau, or the medical social worker at the hospital may be able to help you. The nursing staff will be able to tell you how to get in touch with her or him.

Dentists

Dentists are usually self-employed persons who contract to supply their services to the NHS for a fee. They usually take private, fee-paying patients as well. Your CHC can help you to find a dentist, and a list of dentists is also available at most main post offices, but recommendation by a friend is often the best way to find one. Under the NHS check-ups used to be free but you now pay a small charge; it is still advisable to go for one every six months.

All treatment is free until you're 18, or until you're 19 if you're a student.

All treatment is free until you're 18, or until you're 19 if you're studying. Some other groups of people are also entitled to free treatment, for example if you are unemployed or on a low income, or you are a woman expecting a baby or with a baby under 12 months of age. Leaflet D11 from a post office will explain the details of entitlement to free treatment. When you visit the dentist, tell the receptionist that you want to be treated as an NHS patient, so you don't have to pay charges for private treatment.

Natural teeth are a great asset to your health and looks, and preventive measures are now being emphasised by dentists. Sugar is your teeth's worst enemy, so avoid sugary drinks and sweets. Brushing your teeth correctly is also vital to avoid tooth decay and gum disease. Most people brush their teeth regularly, but it isn't easy to do it properly. Ask your dentist to show you the correct way to brush your teeth when you have a check-up.

Opticians

Opticians are also independent contractors providing some services to the NHS, and most provide private optical services as well. If you think your eyesight isn't as good as it should be, either go to the doctor for an eye test – or walk straight in to the optician and ask for an appointment. Once again, the choice of optician may be through personal recommendation, advice from the CHC or simply the price! Like dental care, eye tests used to be free under the NHS, but you now pay for them, unless you are a full-time student under 19 or are on income support or a low income. Students under 19 and people on income support also get free glasses, and other people on low income may get help towards the cost of a sight test or glasses. Free provision of glasses is limited to the cost of NHS standard lenses, or frames or lenses prescribed by the hospital. Only one NHS frame is totally free. If you choose any other frame you can only get help up to the cost of an NHS frame. If you think you qualify, tell the optician. If applying on low income grounds, ask your optician for form AG1 and send it off to your local social security office. Further information is contained in the leaflet G11, 'NHS Sight Tests and Vouchers for Glasses', from the Post Office, DSS or Citizens Advice Bureau.

The choice of NHS frames is very limited. Many people choose to buy frames and lenses from the large range of designs stocked by opticians. It is worth shopping around as frames and lenses can be very expensive, and contact lenses even more so. It's advisable to take out special insurance (see p.111) if you spend a lot of money on glasses or contact lenses.

Feet

Most foot problems are caused by wearing badly fitting shoes. If you need to see a chiropodist (foot specialist) for corns, callouses or verrucas, make sure there is MChs or SRCh after his or her name, which means that he or she is a State Registered Chiropodist with at least three years' training. NHS chiropody treatment is free for certain groups such as children, people over 60, and the disabled. Most other people have to pay. If you need a chiropodist ask at your local health centre or the CHC.

The Blood Transfusion Service

You can help others by becoming a regular blood donor. All hospitals rely on the transfusion service for emergency blood supplies, and some life-saving drugs are extracted from blood products. Look in the telephone directory under 'Blood Transfusion Service'; they will be very pleased to hear from you. It only takes half an hour and it really is painless!

Services for women

Some health districts have 'Well Women Clinics' specially for women to discuss any health problems or worries, and provide services such as breast examinations, cervical smear tests (cervical cytology) and tests for rubella immunity (see p.186). You can find out whether there are any clinics for women in your area by asking your CHC or Citizens Advice Bureau.

Smear tests

A smear test is a simple early-warning test to see if there are any pre-cancerous cell changes in the neck of the womb (cervix). If there is no well woman clinic in your area, you should still go for regular smear tests to your GP or to your local health authority cytology clinic (ask the CHC or your health clinic where it is) or you may have a smear test at the family planning clinic (see next page). Every woman should go for smear tests once she has started to have sex. The test takes only a few minutes and is quite painless. The doctor takes a sample from the neck of the womb (cervix) which is then sent to a laboratory for analysis. If changes in the cervix are detected at this early pre-cancerous stage then the disease can be cured before it has a chance to develop, which is why it is really important for all women to have a smear test regularly, say every three years.

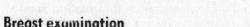

Every woman should go for smear tests once she has started to have sex. The test takes only a few minutes and is quite painless.

Breast examination

When you go to have a smear test the doctor may examine your breasts as well, to check for any lumps or abnormalities. Ask your doctor to show you how to examine your own breasts. Most breast lumps are completely harmless cysts or lumps of fatty tissue, but just occasionally a lump may be the first sign of cancer. That is why it is important to report any changes straight away to your doctor, because the earlier any problems are found the easier it is to treat the disease successfully.

Many women find that their breasts become lumpy and tender around the time of their periods: this is normal. It's best to examine your breasts once a month after a period. It is important to do this properly, and gently or you will feel lumps where there aren't any. Your doctor will show you how to do it properly, and there are plenty of books on the subject too.

Family planning clinics

Health has a social side as well as a physical side. If you feel ready for sex you have a responsibility to yourself and your partner, and should use reliable contraception if you wish to avoid pregnancy. It's also important not to be pressured into anything you don't want. If you trust and care for your partner you can talk things out and avoid any problems (see p.201).

The NHS provides free family planning advice and supplies to anyone, married or single, male or female. You can go to your GP for this service, or to a family planning clinic. Obviously, the time to go for contraception advice is *before* you start to have sex. You can take your partner with you, or go on your own. At the family planning clinic you will be advised on the different methods of contraception and helped to choose the best method for you. Methods of contraception include the pill (combined pill); the mini-pill; the intra-uterine device (IUD, coil); the cap or diaphragm, with spermicide; the sheath or condom (the best-known make is Durex).

If you would like a free leaflet on the different methods of contraception write to the Family Planning Information Service, 27–35 Mortimer Street, London W1N 7RJ (071-636 7866), or you can get information leaflets on contraception from your local family planning clinic or health centre.

Remember that family planning clinics are for men too. You can go for advice, and for supplies of condoms. Anything you discuss at the family planning clinic is confidential and will not be passed on to anyone else without your permission so you can discuss any problems or worries about sex and contraception with the doctor in private. Some clinics have special advice sessions for young people and some are starting 'men only' clinics, staffed exclusively for men. Family planning clinics also provide smear tests for women and some provide pregnancy testing.

You can get the address and time of family planning clinics near you from your health centre, Community Health Council,

Citizens Advice Bureau or information centre, or from the Yellow Pages or telephone directory under 'Family Planning'. Or you can write to the Family Planning Information Service at the address given above.

Brook Advisory Centres provide a free service where young and unmarried people can go for advice and practical help with birth control, pregnancy, sexual and emotional problems. In London, contact them at 233 Tottenham Court Road, London W1P 9AE (071-323 1522 or 071-580 2991). For details of your local Brook Advisory Service, ring the Brook Advisory Centre Information Service on 071–708 1234.

Sexually transmitted diseases (STD)

Sexually transmitted diseases (STD or venereal disease) can be one of the disadvantages of casual sex. You put yourself at risk by having sexual relationships with more than one partner, or with someone who has had sex with more than one partner. There are many different types of sexually transmitted disease, including gonorrhoea (sometimes called 'the clap'), thrush, genital warts, genital herpes, pubic lice ('crabs'), syphilis ('the pox'), or, rarely, AIDS.

For further information get a copy of the booklet 'Guide to a Healthy Sex Life' from your local health education unit, health centre or family planning clinic.

The problem with STD is that it is not always possible to notice symptoms, especially in women. If you have put yourself at risk by having sex with more than one partner, or casual sex with someone you haven't known for very long, or if you suspect that someone you have been with recently has STD, then you should go for a check up at an NHS special clinic. Symptoms might include itching, sores, a lump or rash on the genital area, the anus or in the mouth, increased frequency or pain and discomfort in passing water, any unusual discharge from the vagina, penis or anus.

Special clinics are an entirely confidential service for people of all ages providing diagnosis and treatment of sexually transmitted diseases. If an STD is diagnosed, the staff at the special clinic may ask you for the name and address of people you have recently had sexual intercourse with. They aren't being nosey, but simply want to contact anyone else at risk to prevent the disease from spreading.

To find your local special clinic, look in the phone book under 'Venereal disease', or ask your doctor or Citizens Advice Bureau. You could also phone the casualty department of your local hospital to ask for information, or see the personal column of your local paper.

The best protection against STD is a stable relationship, when both partners are faithful to each other. It is also worth considering, when choosing contraception, that barrier methods such as the condom can have a protective effect against STD. Basic hygiene, washing the genital area before and after sex, can also contribute to prevention.

AIDS

AIDS (Acquired Immune Deficiency Syndrome) has received considerable publicity. It is a condition which prevents the body's defences against illness from working properly, and is thought to be caused by a virus which can be passed on during sex, or through contact with blood that is already infected. Nearly three-quarters of AIDS patients are homosexual or bisexual men, but that does not mean that it cannot be passed on by heterosexual sexual contact. It is also commonly contracted by drug addicts who share a needle with someone who is infected.

It is important to stress that AIDS is a rare condition; on the other hand, as it is so serious the people at risk need to be aware of the danger and it is undoubtedly on the increase. You can be infected with the virus (known as HIV) for years before contracting the disease, but because it attacks the body's defence system itself, once disease occurs it is usually fatal. For further information contact the Terrence Higgins Trust Information Line, 071-833 2971, 7 pm to 10 pm Mondays to Fridays, or write enclosing a large stamped addressed envelope for information to The Terrence Higgins Trust, BM/AIDS, London WC1N 3XX.

Pregnancy

Unwanted pregnancy can be traumatic for all concerned. It is obviously better to avoid pregnancy by using reliable contraception every time you have sex. If your period or your girlfriend's period is overdue and you suspect pregnancy, you should arrange for a pregnancy test as soon as possible. Pregnancy testing can be done by your GP, but can also be done at some family planning clinics and health centres. You can also buy pregnancy testing kits to use at home, although these are quite expensive. If you are pregnant it is vital that you and hopefully your partner as well seek help and advice as soon as possible, from your doctor and your parents, but you can also get confidential help from the Brook Advisory Centre (see p.183) or the British Pregnancy Advisory Service (BPAS).

> **Pregnancy testing can be done by your GP, but can also be done at some family planning clinics and health centres.**

The BPAS is a charitable trust with branches nationwide. It provides a confidential service, pregnancy testing, and counselling, help and advice if you are pregnant. BPAS also provides advice on contraception including 'morning after' contraception. 'Morning after' contraception is for real emergencies only – if your contraception has let you down (for example if a condom breaks during intercourse) or if you have been raped, and treatment must be within 72 hours of intercourse. You can find your local branch listed in the phone book under 'Pregnancy'. Or contact The British Pregnancy Advisory Service,

Austy Manor, Wootton Wawen, Solihull, West Midlands B95 6DA (05642 3225). In addition, there are several other charitable organisations which can provide pregnancy advice; see your local telephone directory under 'Pregnancy'.

Having a baby

Of course, not all young people's pregnancies are unwanted, but it is important to realise the great changes and new responsibilities that having a baby will bring to your life. As well as being a great joy, children can be an emotional and financial burden, so before becoming pregnant you will need to think very carefully whether you and your partner are really ready to have a baby. Statistics show that the least risky age for a woman to have a baby is between 25 and 29; younger women may not have had time to finish their own growing and pregnancy can be exhausting.

If you decide to have a baby, you need to take special care of yourself during pregnancy and take positive health measures. There are lots of inexpensive books on pregnancy and birth, or you could borrow one from the library. Further information on all aspects of pregnancy can be found in *The Pregnancy Book* published by the Health Education Authority. If you are planning to have a baby ask at your health centre, or ask your GP or the Health Visitor at the local child health clinic for a free copy of this excellent publication.

Make sure that you have antibodies against rubella (German measles); your GP can check this. If you contact German measles early in pregnancy your baby could be born with severe mental and physical handicaps, such as deafness, cleft palate, or mental retardation. Try to be immunised against rubella before pregnancy – most girls will have had this done while still at school. If you need to have an injection against rubella, then you should not become pregnant for three months afterwards.

During pregnancy avoid smoking and drinking and try to avoid taking any medicines, even things like aspirin, without getting your doctor's advice first.

Antenatal care

Throughout pregnancy it is very important to have regular checks to ensure that you are both doing well and to prevent anything going wrong. This is known as antenatal care; you will have these at an antenatal clinic at the hospital; or with your own doctor. Your GP will arrange this for you.

When you know you are pregnant you must decide where to have your baby, whether at hospital or at home. Most babies are born in hospital. The advantages of a hospital birth are the immediate availability of expertise and equipment should they be required, but you can discuss all the options with your doctor.

As well as regular antenatal check-ups, antenatal or parentcraft classes are run to help parents in preparation for the birth and looking after the baby. Antenatal or parentcraft classes are usually run by midwives at the hospital or health visitors at your GP's surgery or health centre; these are all free through the NHS. Your GP, midwife or health visitor will be able to advise you on what is available in your area. The National Childbirth Trust also runs classes but there is usually a charge for these.

A midwife will visit you for 10 days after the birth; after that the Health Visitor attached to your doctor's surgery or the local Child Health Clinic will be available for advice on your baby's progress. If you have any problems at home, see the medical social worker before you leave hospital.

Keeping fit and healthy

Most people agree that physical fitness is an important part of health and vitality, not necessarily the pursuit of excellence, but striving for and maintaining a level of fitness to suit you. The Sports Council is very concerned that school leavers tend to abandon sport. A couple of years ago they launched the 'Ever Thought of Sport?' campaign to try to do something to encourage young people to keep up with sport, and to try new forms of exercise. Exercise is fun, and a good way to get out and meet people. It helps to cope with stress, to keep slim and supple, protects the heart and helps you to feel good. (See also 'Using your time' chapter.)

To be beneficial exercise should be regular – half an hour's exercise two or three times a week. It should also be hard enough to make you 'puff and pant' but not gasp for breath. If it's a long time since you did any vigorous exercise, build up gradually. And if you're concerned that exercise might affect any other aspect of your health, for example, if you're recovering from a recent illness or operation, then ask your doctor's advice.

> **To be beneficial exercise should be regular.**

Fitness is basically the ability to do the things that life demands of us. That might be working, continuing education or coping with unemployment and job hunting. Unemployment in itself is a threat to health; if you are unemployed, physical activity is vital to maintain your health and also to help give a structure to the day, contact with people, and to combat stress.

Fit not fat

Exercise and fitness are just part of the whole picture of health. What you put into your body in terms of food is also very important. Don't be obsessed by weight. Faddy diets or 'miracle diets' which claim that you can get by on ridiculously low calorie intakes are not only a threat to health, but are also not effective in the long run.

You have probably read a lot of conflicting advice and information on what we should eat to keep healthy. With so much information around, many people have become confused about food, but in reality the basic rules are simple – eat more fibre, less fat, less sugar and less salt. These recommendations are basically a summary of the NACNE report (National Advisory Committee on Nutrition Education) which represents a concensus of current opinion on food.

The sort of food eaten in the UK and other Western countries tends to contain a lot of fat which is a factor which can lead to heart disease. Try to cut the fat in your diet down by avoiding greasy and fried food, and eating low-fat products like skimmed milk and yoghurt.

Many experts suggest that everyone's health would benefit from almost doubling our intake of natural fibre or roughage. Fibre is found in bread and cereals, potatoes, fruit and leafy vegetables. Natural fibre keeps the digestive system working properly and prevents constipation, so that harmful materials are eliminated from the body quickly.

One of the problems of industrialisation and the development of food technology over the last century was the change to refined and over-processed foods. Diseases such as constipation, bowel cancer and piles became common in the western world. High amounts of fibre can protect against these and many other ailments, and are an important part of any properly balanced diet.

Sugar has no nutritional value other than its energy content. It contains a high amount of calories (energy) and taking in too many calories for the amount of energy you expend leads to weight gain. Sugar is also a major cause of tooth decay. Look closely at the labels of convenience foods – even savoury foods like baked beans have sugar added.

Salt is associated with high blood pressure, a risk factor for heart disease. Much processed food already contains a high proportion of salt so, again, read food labels carefully and try not to add too much of it to your own cooking.

Your weight

If you stick to the guidelines above, and exercise regularly, your weight should take care of itself. Healthy, balanced eating is the only way to keep slim in the long run. If you feel that you need to lose weight, your first step should be to consult your doctor, who can give you sound advice, and refer you to a dietician or slimmers' group if she or he really feels it is necessary.

Don't always gauge your ideal weight from a weight chart; these can be misleading, as it is the percentage of body fat which is most important. A quarter of the population in their twenties is overweight, that is, carrying around excess fat. Losing fat is the key to sustained weight loss. Unfortunately, weight loss is not necessarily fat loss. Crash diets may produce rapid loss in weight but what goes is body water, muscle and organ tissue rather than excess fat.

Girls are particularly at risk over fad dieting – one recent study concluded that one in every 100 girls over 16 has severe anorexia nervosa and that many other girls in this age group at some time resort to severe slimming, weight loss and vomiting after eating. Needless to say, this is a threat to health – depriving the body of adequate supplies of nutrients at a time of growth and development. It's sad that society and the media put so much pressure on girls to follow a particular image of 'looking good' at all costs. Talk to your doctor or someone else you trust in confidence if you think you or someone you know is dieting in a way that is dangerous to health.

Eating at home

If you live with your parents or with friends, everyone in the home can contribute to buying, choosing and preparing food. Safeguard yourself by eating a healthy diet most of the time – don't worry about the occasional lapses. If other people in the household want to eat cream cakes and chips all day, it doesn't mean you have to.

If you're leaving home to live on your own for the first time it can be all too easy to live on junk food. Make a point of eating a good main meal every day, based on the guidelines given earlier. It *is* possible to eat well on a shoestring – providing you do your shopping sensibly and plan carefully. There are hundreds of really delicious recipes for healthy eating – look for wholefood recipe books in your local library. And remember that eating is a pleasure – why not share it with friends?

Drugs

Society in this country is extremely drug-orientated. We grow up with the view that there's a 'pill for every ill', a view that is encouraged by widespread advertising. We take painkillers at the first sign of a headache, tobacco or alcohol or tranquillisers, when we're feeling low. All drugs used for non-medical purposes, whether legal or illegal, are almost always taken as a prop – a chemical crutch to get through the day when feeling down, or to make social life go with more of a swing. Most people start to take drugs because of social pressure – usually from friends. You know the situation – you were with a group of people who were smoking, somebody offered you a cigarette and it was difficult to refuse. The same is true of other drugs; people try them because their friends do, or out of curiosity, and suddenly they're hooked, addicted.

Smoking

People start to smoke at school, often intending to give up after a year or two, only to find that the powerful addictive properties of nicotine are too much for them.

If you smoke, try to do something about giving it up now, as it gets harder as the years go by. Action to stop people smoking would do more to improve health in this country than any other single measure. Smoking is a rip-off. The Government makes £11.5 million every day from tobacco taxation. The tobacco industry makes billions of pounds at the expense of people who smoke. Even apart from the very serious health risks, smoking is just not worth it – you'll smell foul, stain your teeth and fingers, and pay through the nose for the privilege. Think what you could do with the money – between £500 and £800 a year for an average smoker.

Alcohol

Apart from cigarettes, alcohol is the other major non-medical legal drug. The difference in terms of health risk is that whilst it is always dangerous to smoke cigarettes, alcohol can be taken in moderation with no apparent harmful effects. In medical terms 'moderation' means two or three standard drinks two or three times a week for men, and slightly less for women. One standard drink is half a pint of ordinary beer or lager, a single 1/6 gill of spirits, one glass of wine, a small glass of sherry, or a measure of vermouth or aperitif.

> **66**
>
> **Alcohol always affects your judgement even if you think you are perfectly all right.**
>
> **99**

Even if you don't exceed these recommended limits, don't forget there are times when even a small amount of alcohol is dangerous. For example, you shouldn't drink if you are taking certain medicines (ask your doctor about this when you get a prescription). You should never drink before operating machinery or before driving a car or a motorbike. Alcohol always affects your judgement even if you think you are perfectly all right. *Never* drink and drive – it's not just your life you're putting at risk.

Illegal drugs

Both legal and illegal drugs can be abused, though many people only think of drug abuse and drug problems in terms of illegal ones. Both legal and illegal drugs can damage your health permanently, and can cause many social problems and bad experiences.

Illegal drugs can be loosely divided into three groups – stimulants, narcotics and hallucinogens. Stimulants include cocaine and amphetamines which, as the name suggests, produce a 'high', an alert feeling through stimulating the nervous system. Narcotics include morphine and heroin, derived from the opium poppy. They are both extremely powerful, addictive drugs, which are very dangerous, damaging to health, and often have side effects such as nausea and vomiting. Hallucinogens include cannabis (marijuana). This is a mild hallucinogen, said to be non-addictive. LSD or 'acid' is also an hallucinogenic drug, as is Ecstacy, which also includes stimulants. Crack, a pure form of cocaine, although not strictly a narcotic, is every bit as addictive as heroin, possibly more so.

The only way to safeguard yourself from having a bad experience, damaging your health or developing a habit is never to take drugs. But many people do take legal or illegal drugs at some time in their lives. If you are offered something, don't take it if you feel 'down', depressed or worried. Maybe you'll think it's the answer at the time; but this is the worst thing to do. Never take drugs on your own or with people you don't know very well or don't trust. Avoid powerful addictive drugs. Drugs bought illegally may contain other substances and you can never really be sure how strong the drug is, so the effect might be stronger than anticipated. Mixing drugs of any kind is extremely dangerous, particularly combinations of alcohol and other depressants such as tranquillisers (see next page). Mixing alcohol and painkillers is also very dangerous.

Apart from the risks involved with drugs themselves, the act of injecting can itself lead to problems such as overdosing, transmission of infections such as AIDS or hepatitis, and septic infections caused by unsterile needles. Injecting drugs is more likely to lead to dependence.

Getting help

If you think your use of drugs is becoming a problem or if you are worried about a friend, your local Citizens Advice Bureau will be able to advise you in confidence of any self-help groups in the area, or whether the local health authority has their own counselling service and Drug Dependency Unit. You can also contact SCODA (Standing Conference on Drug Abuse) for information, at 1–4 Hatton Place, London EC1N 8ND (071-430 2341)

Tranquillisers

Many people have taken tranquillisers or sleeping pills (barbiturates) at some time in their lives. Sometimes tranquillisers such as valium and librium, or anti-depressants, are prescribed by doctors for a short time to ease the pain of a distressing event, depression and anxiety. Whilst they can be invaluable in some cases and effective in the short term, in the long term they can cause problems. The original cause of the unhappiness may still be there, and there is a risk of addiction with regular use. It can be very difficult and distressing for people to come off these drugs, and it is important to withdraw from them gradually. In some areas there are tranquilliser groups to support people going through this experience. MIND (the National Association for Mental Health) can provide help and advice on this and on many other emotional problems. Their address is 22 Harley Street, London W1N 2ED (071-637 0741) (branches throughout the UK).

Many doctors are now trying to introduce more 'treatment through talking' rather than prescribing drugs for emotional problems. They try to help a patient to solve or come to terms with a problem through talking it out through psychotherapy or counselling.

Mental health

Mental health is every bit as important as physical health, and emotional pain can be as bad if not worse than physical pain. If you feel very low, depressed or anxious, or if you know someone who does, then seek help. MIND can help with information and advice, and you can consult your GP. Everyone has to face problems, stresses and pressures, and sometimes these can seem too much to bear. Seek help for emotional problems just as you would for a broken arm. And remember that if someone you know is going through this sort of problem, they will need all the help, support and encouragement you can give.

Alternative medicine

Many people find that their mental health and well-being are improved or maintained by yoga and relaxation techniques. Yoga is also sometimes used as an alternative therapy for some stress-related illnesses. Alternative medicine is the name given to a variety of practices like acupuncture or homeopathy. There are many of these therapies and they seem to be attracting more interest but it should be pointed out that there is little hard statistical evidence on the benefits of alternative therapies as opposed to conventional medicine. Some people seek alternative therapies to complement their conventional medical treatment. Some forms of healing such as acupuncture and the Alexander Technique aim to cure the whole being, not just the physical body, and so are known as 'holistic'.

Homeopathy

Homeopathy uses special remedies to stimulate the body's own healing power, usually minute doses of extracts derived from plants and minerals. It is one of the few alternative therapies available within the NHS, although there are not many practitioners. Usually homeopathic doctors run private clinics for which you have to pay, but many will offer reduced fees if you have a low income.

Acupuncture

Acupuncture is a very old form of traditional Chinese medicine which is now practised in the West, having been brought to Europe in the last century. It involves the use of very fine sterilised needles inserted at certain points of the body along the 'meridian' or pathways of 'vital energy' which are said to run beneath the surface. An acupuncturist will charge a fee.

Osteopathy and chiropractic

Osteopaths and chiropractors deal largely with back and joint pain and related disorders. Both use manipulation therapy techniques including massage and pressure to correct common musculo-skeletal complaints. Some orthopaedic surgeons and physiotherapists within the NHS are collaborating with osteopaths and campaigning to bring them into the NHS. Like homeopaths, they charge for their services, but may reduce the fee for needy cases.

Hypnotherapy

Hypnotherapy has been more widely used recently for a variety of problems such as smoking, anxiety and obesity. It involves the use of hypnosis to release tension and stress. Again a charge is made for a course of treatment.

Yoga

Many people in this country practise yoga, and recently research has been undertaken into its therapeutic effects as a means of improving mental and physical health. It has a well documented stress-reducing effect and has been reported as having a beneficial effect in treatment of anxiety, tobacco addiction, dependence on tranquillisers, alcoholism, back pain and many other disorders. There are many good yoga classes run privately or by local education authorities; ask at your library for details (see also p. 238).

If you are interested in any aspect of medicine, whether alternative or within the NHS, contact the College of Health, 2 Marylebone Road, London NW1 (071-935 3251). It is a non-profit-making institution offering information, education and advice on keeping yourself healthy, how to deal with common ailments and what self-help groups can offer, how to make the best use of the health service, and how to find qualified practitioners in a variety of alternative therapies.

R ELATIONSHIPS

Relationships between people are the most attractive, treacherous, worrying, mysterious and wonderful aspect of being alive. No hand-book can give you hard and fast rules about how to conduct them in order to avoid heart ache, jealousy or disappointment. How to relate to others is something we learn day in day out from cradle, play-pen, playground and disco through to factory floor, university, college canteen and cinema queue . . . the list is endless. Everywhere we go we relate to others.

While there are no hard and fast rules, there are things that are worth pointing out, but given the obvious limitations on space here there are bound to be subjects left undiscussed. The list of addresses and books on p.245 may help you with other problems about relationships.

Yes sir no sir

When you leave school you'll probably go to work, on to further education or to higher education, on to a Youth Training scheme place, or even take off and see the world. You will make new friends and come into contact with new forms of authority. By now you've had plenty of practice with new friends and with authority figures in school. But your experience of an employer or manager, a benefits officer or YTS leader may be limited. In nearly all relationships there is to a greater or lesser degree a power struggle. Very few of us achieve equality without some kind of struggle. Those in authority over you will perhaps treat you well, respect your individuality and your adult status. Others may not. You could find yourself frustrated by the attitudes of those in authority who may seem quick to patronise, exploit or disapprove. The trick is to learn the wisdom of restraint and arm yourself with the facts. Rather than raise your voice in righteous indignation immediately you feel yourself wronged and find yourself out on your ear, keep cool. Check out your rights in the situation. If appropriate see your union representative (and if you aren't in a union find out about joining one – see p.25), or see your local Law Centre or Citizens Advice Bureau.

Humanity has managed to split itself into different classes, castes and hierarchies, and this means that there are gaps in understanding between us. Old and young are mutually suspicious, boss and worker mutually wary. Watch the balance of power and remember that whoever you may be in conflict with is human too. Politeness goes a long way and is in your interest, and it *isn't* the same as crawling. There is a tendency to expect conflict between generations but it doesn't have to be that way. There's no reason why people of different age, sex, creed or colour can't co-exist harmoniously.

The age of consent

Once you're 16 you've reached the age of consent, except in Northern Ireland, where it is 17. (Did you know you can also sell scrap metal, buy fireworks and liqueur chocolates?) The age of consent means you can legally agree to have sexual relationships. It doesn't mean you *have* to have sex. The age of consent was originally designed to protect girls from sexual exploitation. Men sometimes think that because a girl reaches 16 she ought to be ready and willing. Not so. Boys too cannot legally consent to sex until they are 16, and a woman could be accused of indecent assault if she had sex with a boy under that age.

Reaching the age of consent doesn't mean you have to think of yourself as heterosexual either. Heterosexual means that you only feel attracted to the opposite sex, but not everybody is heterosexual. Even so there is still a lot of prejudice about sexuality and most people are expected to be heterosexual. Lots of people are homosexual, which means they are attracted to their own sex, or bi-sexual, which means they fancy people of both sexes. Some people feel sure at an early age of how they are sexually, others go through changes and phases, many feel confused and worried. In the end however it is a matter of personal choice. (See also p.203.)

There is more public attention paid to young people with regard to their sexuality than just about any other aspect of their lives. There is also a lot of confusing sexual pressure on them which leads to unnecessary hang-ups. The world says conflicting things. In one voice it says sex outside marriage is dirty, naughty, wicked and rude, and in another voice it encourages sexiness and the expression of sexuality. Very confusing. Nobody should get involved in a sexual relationship unless they really want to, are ready for the consequences and are properly protected against unwanted pregnancy.

There is a lot of confusing sexual pressure which leads to unnecessary hang-ups.

You are well advised to avoid having sex to be part of the crowd, or to be like people in adverts, pop videos, movies and so on. Never have sex because a partner threatens to leave you if you won't. You're better off without someone who tries to exert that kind of power and pressure over you. It is foolish to have sex because everyone else you know seems to have experienced it.

There is a fashionable media image striding across the pages of magazines and towering over us on bill-boards, of a young woman who appears to be free, sexy, wealthy, attractive, aggressive, blonde, tanned and very slim. She is happy and powerful, gets the guy, the job, the house, the yacht and holds the future in the palm of her hand. There's a macho male version too. Most of us aren't like them, but that doesn't mean we don't make the grade. It means we're all different and attractive in our own way. The Chinese used to bind girls' feet at birth to make them tiny, which was a sign of beauty. In later life those women were almost crippled. Similarly trying to copy images of beauty can cause awful and unnecessary hang-ups.

Sexual relationships can be wonderful but also treacherous. They are unlike other relationships because they nearly always imply a new kind of emotional complication. Treat them with caution, wisdom and a little awe. Times have changed and attitudes to sexual relationships have relaxed, but there is still a lot of prejudice and the double standards still operate. Boys who get around are still regarded as Romeos and Casanovas, and while the older generation may wag its finger, it chuckles and says boys will be boys. If girls flout sexual convention they run the risk of being called not Romeo or Juliet, but 'old slag' or 'old dog', even by the boys with whom they are involved. Similarly girls who refuse to have sex with boyfriends run the risk of being called 'tight' or 'frigid', words never applied to boys. Boys have other pressures to cope with. If they aren't macho, they are in danger of being called wimps, poofs and weeds. None of it is fair. A wise person keeps an eye on these conflicts and avoids them as much as possible.

With luck and a bit of judgement you may avoid all the dangers and be involved in a balanced, committed and loving relationship. Commitment can generate great happiness, especially if it's never taken for granted. It's impossible to define what love and falling in love are all about. All I would say is when you find it, don't shackle it. Jealousy and possessiveness strangle love.

Loneliness

One of the spin-offs of the media images of the successful young person, the striding girl and the tough young man – strong, silent and infinitely capable – makes some people feel that if they're (a) not like that and (b) not in a couple, they are social failures. Not at all! Sometimes a vicious circle sets in. You don't have a boy or girlfriend. Your gang are all in couples. You stop going out. You retire mournfully to your bedroom. But that doesn't help anybody. The way out of loneliness is to get out there and find others of like mind. Others, remember, are looking for you too. Millions of people feel lonely. Grit your teeth and bend your will, choose a hobby or activity, a sport or evening class, a youth club or dramatic society, somewhere where you will meet others with a common focus (see p. 232 for suggestions). You have nothing to lose but your isolation.

Rejection

Falling in love, becoming sexually involved or going out with someone, invite a certain amount of emotional risk. At any time, whatever your gender, whether you are gay or straight, you run the risk of rejection or loss. It is always painful and rocks your confidence. If it's a major break-up it feels really devastating. Life will never be the same again. You'll never, never love anyone again. And it feels like that for a while. But you come through it, you realise it may even have been a good thing, as break-ups and rejections aren't necessarily disasters.

A rejection doesn't mean you're less of a person; if someone rejects you, remember you may have done it to somebody else. The trick is never to let one other person be the centre of your universe. Always have an independent life, your own friends and interests; never submerge your individuality in another person so that if you lose him or her you are paralysed.

Contraception and pregnancy

If you choose to have sex, make sure you are protected against unwanted pregnancy. Go to the doctor, family planning clinic or Brook Advisory Centre for contraception advice (see p.183 for details). And although this is mainly addressed to girls, because they're the ones that get pregnant, boys have just as much responsibility. A considerate boyfriend offers to go to the clinic with his girlfriend.

Coitus Interruptus (withdrawal method) and the Safe Period are both about as safe as a condom full of holes. Don't rely on these so called 'methods'.

The unexpected pregnancy

If you think you are pregnant, don't panic – worry can delay a period. See your doctor or family planning clinic and ask for a pregnancy test (see p. 185). Share your anxiety with someone you trust who can advise, comfort and support you. Nobody should ever be forced into having a child, giving up a child for adoption or terminating a pregnancy. It must be a girl's or woman's own decision, although it is very helpful to have someone open-minded with whom to discuss all the pros and cons. From the age of 16 it is up to the individual to decide whether or not she continues with a pregnancy and if she decides to have an abortion she will not need her parents' consent. However, it's always best to involve parents if at all possible. There are pregnancy counselling services and agencies listed on pp. 241–2.

Thinking about marriage

At 16 you can leave home with your parents' or guardian's permission. In law, however, you are in the custody of your parents until you're 18 (see p.130). Under 18, you can only get married with the consent of your parents, guardians or, if parents are divorced, the permission of whoever has custody. There are fewer teenage marriages than there were ten years or so ago, but of those who do marry very young, an alarming number split up within a few years. Marriage is a major step; it involves legal and emotional commitments to your partner and to any children you may have. If you want to live with someone without getting married, the same rules apply.

Young people who have been born and brought up in the UK

but whose parents grew up in a different society and environment often find themselves in conflict on many levels – religious, cultural, sexual, political and so on. There are no easy answers but don't be afraid to ask for help, support and advice. Through local agencies you can track down various forms of counselling. For example, the Asian Women's Resource Centre (see p. 241 for address) can help Asian girls and women, providing counselling, support, sympathy and comfort. There are also refuges for Asian women who want to leave home due to family conflict.

On being gay

For homosexual men the age of consent for sex is 21 (although in practice few prosecutions are brought where both partners are over 18 and are consenting to the relationship). Lesbianism is not against the law at any age. Despite the liberalising power of the gay and feminist movements of the last fifteen years or so, there is still a lot of narrow-minded prejudice about homosexuality. This causes terrible anxiety to men and women of all ages. People with homosexual feelings are afraid to express them and suffer in intolerable silence. There are organisations which can help, advise, support and comfort people who need help, details of which are on pp. 241–2

Despite the liberalising power of the gay and feminist movements, there is still a lot of narrow-minded prejudice about homosexuality.

Rape

The picture painted in this chapter so far may seem to present an image of sexual relationship as a battlefield or board game where conflict, prejudice and heartbreak are the inevitable outcome. Of course it need not all be like that. But it's pointless pretending that humanity has worked itself out sexually any more than it has politically, socially or economically, and it's when things go wrong that people need help. For example, criminal sexuality has not gone away nor does it appear to be on its way out. Sex is only dirty when it's the result of attack or coercion, or when it's sold for a profit. The dirtiest of all sex is sexual assault or rape.

Rape and assault are crimes that every girl and woman fears, and boys and men are also, although less frequently, victims. There are some idiotic preconceptions about rape. There is a suspicion in some people's minds that a rape victim 'must have asked for it'. She was alone with a man, they say, or she wore a low cut dress or a short skirt. There is a slogan from the women's movement which sets the record straight: 'Whatever we wear, wherever we go, yes means yes and no means no.'

Part of the problem is that male aggression is so much in evidence in the media, much of which suggests that women enjoy violence. But there is a world of difference between the rough and tumble of some love-making and an unwanted attack by someone intent on forcing another person to have sex against their will. If you are the victim of sexual assault (which can mean *any* form of sexual coercion) or rape, it is *never* your fault. Don't feel you have to hide the experience and suffer the trauma in silence. Find someone in whom you can confide and contact Rape Crisis as soon as you are able to (071-837 1600).

There are obvious ways of reducing the risk of being raped. Avoid being left alone with someone you don't fully trust. Don't walk alone in the dark in lonely, badly-lit alleys, lanes or estates. Some people find that taking a course in self-defence helps them feel more confident and safer when alone. Reporting the attack to the police can be one of the most distressing after-effects, but it *is* important. However, consult Rape Crisis first if you can and they will advise you on the procedures. But remember if you want to tell the police you should do so as soon as possible, as delay may go against your case.

Incest

Incest strictly speaking means having sex with your father, mother, son, daughter, brother, sister, grandmother or grandfather. It is illegal. Some of the organisations involved in helping incest victims regard all forms of sexual abuse or interference by an older person in authority as incest.

It is a very complex issue and is maybe even more taboo as a subject for discussion than homosexuality. The original taboo was founded on the belief that children born of incestuous relationships were likely to be deformed or retarded, and there is truth in this.

Incest is far more common than people realise. This is because its victims are among the most silent and secretive of all who feel they have something to hide. They feel ashamed, blame themselves, agonise because they may not have resisted. They fear telling anyone because they don't want to disrupt their families. It is important to find someone in whom to confide, someone who can reassure you it's not your fault and there is no need for guilt. The guilty ones are the relatives who corrupt the innocence of others and force themselves on younger members of the family, even raping them. There are some victims who resist, some who in confusion and innocence participate unwillingly, and those who are perhaps actively and willingly involved in an incestuous relationship.

Anyone who has anxieties about incest in any way should contact one of the organisations listed on p.241. Don't hesitate to ask for help if the incest happened a long time ago. A lot of people don't feel they are able to talk about it until years afterwards.

GETTING AROUND

We all need to travel regularly, even if it's only down to the shops to buy a pint of milk. Wherever you want to go, whether it's getting around in your own neighbourhood or flying to exotic places, there are always different ways of doing it. In assessing which is the best for you there might be conflicting considerations; for example, although air travel is quicker (and often cheaper) for long distances than going overland, you miss out on seeing the country that you're travelling through. Also, there are often rules and regulations that exclude the obvious way of getting there, for example, about booking in advance; though it is sometimes possible to bend or avoid them. So whether planning your holiday or thinking of the best way of going shopping, it's advisable to know all the alternatives.

Public transport

Some local transport authorities provide special reduced-rate passes for young people provided that you are still in full-time education. For example, you can travel to school or college for 14p in Manchester up to the age of 19 if at school or college, providing you have the requisite pass (your school or college will tell you how to get it). If you travel regularly along the same route, you will find that in most areas it is cheaper to buy some form of season ticket (these are irrespective of age). For example, in Newcastle you save about 25 per cent on your fares on the bus and metro with a season ticket, and London Regional Transport offers bus, bus-and-tube, and all-service passes that cost the same or less than the total for return journeys during the working week, so any extra journeys you make – in the evening or weekend – become free. It is often cheaper to travel out of the rush hour; if you make a return journey that starts after a certain time in the morning (usually 9.30 am) both British Rail and London Regional Transport will sell you a cheap day return that gives you a substantial saving.

Trains

British Rail are currently offering the Young Person's Railcard, which offers you cheap rail travel for £15, two passport-sized photos, and proof that you're under 24. Most other tickets are then two-thirds price. The catches are that there are minimum fares (£3 single or cheap day return, £6 others) before 10 am on weekdays, except in July and August and on bank holidays. You can't use it on trains not operated by British Rail, on special excursions, 'Nightrider' and boat trains, or services leaving Kings Cross between 1.55 pm and 7.01 pm on Fridays.

For continental travel British Rail sell the Inter-Rail Card, which offers unlimited rail travel for one month in 22 countries for around £55. It also gives you free travel on some European ferries, plus a few other concessions. You will have to pay a little extra for some of the luxury services, eg the TGV between Marseilles and Paris. If your constitution is robust enough, you can even use it to save on overnight accommodation by sleeping on a night train.

If you're only going to a few places on the Continent, you may find you can get discounts from certain travel agents; it is worth looking around for bargains.

Bus and coach travel

National Express are the biggest coach operators in Britain, with a country-wide network. On long distance routes they offer a basic service, or, for a slightly higher fare, the Rapide service with fewer stops, in-coach toilets, and hostess service for light refreshments. Young people can buy a Coach Card for £5.00, which entitles you to travel at about two-thirds of the full price, but not on the Rapide services. There is more competition on Scottish routes, and information on these can be got from the individual operators. At full fare, coaches are cheaper than trains, but if you have a Young Person's Railcard you should compare rail and coach fares for any journey you are planning.

For more local services, there is no central information point on fares or schedules, and you have to contact the individual operators. 'Explorer' tickets are available which allow you to travel as often as required on any one operator's buses.

Bus travel to Europe can be uncomfortable on longer journeys (and can cost more if you take food and time into account). There is also the danger of using an unlicensed service which has no restraint on driver's hours or bus maintenance. The main legitimate operators are Supabus (part of National Express), Euroways, or City Sprint (part of Hoverspeed), all of which can be booked through travel agents.

Walking

Walking isn't talked about much in terms of getting people from place to place – is this because you don't need to buy anything to do it? Yet despite this stunning lack of publicity, more than a third of all journeys are made entirely on foot – and even a quarter of all journeys to work. When you consider that in the centre of a large city the door-to-door travel speed of car users can be around 5 km per hour, walking may even be the faster option.

66

More than a third of all journeys are made entirely on foot.

99

If you're interested in walking holidays there are many long-distance paths – for example, the Pennine Way or the Ridgeway Path – that take several days or even weeks to travel. They avoid towns and can give you a wonderful sense of being away from it all. You do not have to be an excellent cross-country navigator as there are detailed guide-books for both the long-distance paths and shorter countryside rambles, and you do not have to camp out either if you do not wish to, as the guidebooks tell you where you can get information on cheap places to spend the night. Some of these long-distance paths are shown on Ordnance Survey maps. They are also generally well signposted, but with occasional omissions.

Cycling

Cycling can often be a fast as well as a cheap way of getting about. Not only that, it keeps you fit and doesn't pollute the surroundings with noise or fumes. Some people think cycling is too dangerous, which is a pity, because with a bit of care it can be almost as safe as a car for comparable journeys.

Buying a bike

A new bike will cost anything from £90 upwards, with a second-hand one starting from £30 for a roadworthy single-speed. Where you buy from is almost as important as what make you get, as a good cycle shop will advise you on size, make and accessories, and provide back-up service when something goes wrong. Ask around for recommendations as to the sort of bike you want; if nobody can help you, or you're buying an expensive one, swot up on a good bicycle book. However, don't be bullied into getting a five or 10-speed bike if you just want a hack bike that will take you from A to B and not require too much maintenance; a three-speed with Sturmey Archer hub gears will probably be all you need.

The extras

It's a legal requirement to have lights, both front and back, if you use your bike at night. You can get either battery-powered lights or dynamo lights (costing from £10) which run off electricity generated by the bike's movement, but they need a battery back-up unit (Pifco do one) that provides power when the dynamo stops. Other useful (and occasionally essential) bits include a good quality lock (bikes are a favourite target for thieves), carrier, horn, mudflap, trouser clips, tool kit and wet weather clothing. As well as lights, a rear reflector is required at night by law, but other reflective gear, for example a fluorescent Sam Browne belt, is good for getting you noticed (and avoided) by motorists when it's dark.

Riding tips

If you haven't cycled since childhood it's worth doing a little planning before heading off into rush-hour traffic. Plan a route that avoids as far as possible danger spots such as roundabouts, and if you can get an experienced cyclist to accompany you on your first few journeys, so much the better. Try not to wobble about; cars can avoid you more effectively if you travel straight and give hand signals before changing direction. Most accidents happen near junctions, so be especially careful when you travel through them. Read the Highway Code and follow what it says.

Repairs

Avoid repairs as much as possible by maintaining your bike regularly; a bit of oil on the chain and bearings every fortnight and keeping the tyres pumped up hard can save you a lot of trouble later. Keep an eye on the brakes, adjusting them, oiling the cables and renewing the brake blocks when worn. However, you will never entirely avoid carrying out some repairs to your machine; if you don't want to go to a bicycle repair shop you can probably find a local night class on bicycle repair, or else read a good bicycle repair guide.

Cycles and public transport

You may not want to begin your cycling journey from home, so in theory taking your bike on public transport is the ideal way of getting to your starting point if you don't have access to a car. You can take bikes on trains, but unfortunately, British Rail has complex rules covering when and where you can do this. These are given in their 'Cycles on Trains' leaflet (available from stations and Travelcentres), or else you can ring their local inquiry number for details.

You can't take a cycle on buses and coaches unless you can disguise it as a suitcase.

Organisations

There are two organisations of particular help to cyclists. The Cycle Campaign Network is a meeting point for groups campaigning for a better deal for cyclists. It has groups around the country, the largest of which provide insurance, advice, discounts at cycle shops and publications. Contact the Network, c/o The London Cycling Campaign, 3 Stamford Street, London SE1 9NT (071-928 7220) for details of the group nearest you. The Cyclists' Touring Club, 69 Meadrow, Godalming, Surrey (04868 7217), is the largest British cycling organisation, and provides insurance services, touring advice and legal help.

Travelling abroad

Before going abroad it's worth doing a little research on the country you're visiting, even if all you do Is skim a guide book; being unprepared might not just lead to shocks, it can also be expensive. For example, if you arrive in a country on a public holiday with no local currency you may find that it is difficult to get some and costs a lot to do so. Most tourist destinations have offices in London, and occasionally in other cities, that will load you down with useful (and useless) pamphlets. A phrase book or dictionary can be very helpful, as outside tourist areas most locals don't speak anything but their own language. You can get local maps from a specialist dealer – the biggest range is available from Stanford's, Long Acre, London WC2 (071-836 7863).

If you're a student, take an ISIC (International Student Identity Card). This enables you to get discounts on many flights, hotels, galleries, museums and cinemas. Even if a discount isn't advertised, do ask for it. You are eligible for the card if you are studying for more than 15 hours a week for more than six months a year. It costs £3.50, lasts for a year, and comes on the back of the NUS card, but you have to pay and provide a passport type photograph to get it validated at your student union or the local student travel agencies.

Whether you travel alone, or as part of a group, depends on what you expect from your journey. Travelling alone is more dangerous but it forces you to get to know the locals. In groups, you are far less prone to the depression (and elation) that strikes you on your own, but it insulates you to some extent from the country you are travelling in. If you travel with one or two other people you might well strike a happy balance.

For details of cheap rail and bus travel abroad, see pp. 207-8.

Insurance

It's always worth taking out travel insurance. Although in countries in the EC (France, Germany, Holland, Greece, Italy, Belgium, Denmark, Luxembourg, Ireland, Spain, Portugal), you are entitled to whatever the locals get in the way of free medical treatment, this may not be very much, and even if there is a free national health service, often the paperwork and bureaucracy involved doesn't make it worthwhile for the visitor. (If you're still interested, get form E111 from the Department of Health.)

Get a policy that covers you for medical expenses (which should be at least £200,000 for travel in the USA, £20,000 in Europe), for the loss of personal belongings and money, and for personal accident. On package holidays and long flights using cheap tickets, it's worth insuring against missing the flight because of accident, illness, or other cause. The costs of insurance vary according to where you travel, the amount of cover, and how long it is for, but for a fortnight's holiday in Europe you can expect to pay between £8 and £16. Don't just take whatever policy your travel agent offers; most insurance companies, banks, and insurance brokers (see p. 111) offer what may be a better deal.

Motorists going abroad are no longer legally required to get a

Green Card from their insurance company for continental travel but it is strongly recommended; this provides the same cover as you have in the UK, but without it your insurance cover will be inferior to third-party only. It costs £20–£30 from your insurance company, though some provide them free. In Spain you will also require a Bail Bond, which you should be able to get from your insurance company as well. There are other insurance deals for motorists such as the AA Five Star, which undertake to get you home if your car breaks down.

Passports, visa, and identity cards

If you're leaving the country, you will need some form of official document before the country you want to visit will let you in. The usual one is a passport, but there are alternatives if you're not travelling all that far or frequently.

A full passport costs £15 and lasts for ten years if you are over 18, five years if under. It is valid for all countries. You can get an application form from a post office and have to submit it with two identical photographs of yourself. These have to be of a specified size (50mm x 38 mm – photo booths produce them in the required dimensions) and one must be countersigned (as must the form) by someone who knows you and is in one of the professions – eg a doctor, schoolteacher, JP or minister of religion. If you are under 18 you also have to have your parents' consent. Allow about four weeks, especially in summer, for your application to be processed.

If you're sure you're not going to go overseas more than once in the next ten years, then a British Visitor's passport is cheaper and quicker to get than a passport. You can get one on the spot from a main post office and it costs £7.50. It is valid for one year. You need two recent photos, as for a passport, plus a birth certificate and another form of identification. It is valid for most holiday destinations.

If you're only going to France, there is another option – the British Excursion Document, which is obtainable from a post office for £2. It involves the same requirements as to photos and paperwork as the British Visitor's passport. It is only valid for a month, and will only cover you for trips of up to 60 hours in France, so it's all right for a day trip. For day trips to Belgium you can use a special identity card, which your travel agent should be able to help you arrange.

For many countries a passport is all you need. However, for some places you also need a visa, which is a sort of personal permission to visit the country, and is usually shown in the form of a stamp in your passport. You definitely need one for Australia and the USSR, and for any other country outside Western Europe you should find out several weeks before you go whether one is necessary – a travel agent will be able to tell you. They are no longer required for the USA. If you are going on a tour, the tour operator will arrange it; otherwise get your travel agent to do it, or contact the relevant embassy in London.

Taking money abroad

When you go abroad you could just stuff your pockets with pounds sterling and rely on changing them into the currency of the country you are visiting, but you would be asking to have your money stolen. And while you may have little difficulty in changing it, you will get poor rates of exchange. Going to a bank or 'bureau de change' before you leave this country and getting money in the currency you require will solve the problem of changing it, but will make you an even more tempting target for a thief abroad. There are, however, ways of taking money without involving this risk, but they all cost something.

Banks issue traveller's cheques which come in fixed denominations, like banknotes, and can be got in most major trading currencies – eg dollars, pounds, Swiss francs and German marks. You exchange them for currency in practically any bank overseas; many hotels also accept them. Their main advantage is that if you lose them, refunds can often be arranged on the spot. They cost about 1 per cent of their face value (except to customers of some building societies), but you do get a better rate of exchange than cash. Your bank will be able to supply you with them, but may require notice if you want them in a currency other than sterling. If you do not have a bank account you can buy them from the foreign exchange till of any bank.

Credit cards such as Access and Visa can be very useful as back-ups to traveller's cheques, and can even be used to get money from overseas banks.

If you're travelling in some parts of Europe and you've got a bank account, you can use Eurocheques. These are very similar to ordinary cheques, except that you can write them in foreign currencies. You have to have a special cheque card to go with them that costs around £8 for a year. It doubles as a cash dispenser card in Spain and France, and there are plans to extend this facility elsewhere. Whether you should use them in Continental cash machines is another peril; if the machine refuses to give you your card back you not only fail to get the money you needed at that moment, but you also cannot use your cheques. If you're going to the USA, take dollar traveller's cheques, as they probably won't accept anything else outside the major cities, and even there you will have problems changing sterling traveller's cheques.

If you're travelling in countries off the beaten track, a combination of dollars (kept in a moneybelt) and American Express traveller's cheques should be enough. In case of emergencies, you can go to a local bank and have them telex your bank which will then guarantee to refund the local bank the specific sum of money you ask for. In some countries however this can take several weeks and will be expensive. You can go to British embassies or consulates if you are destitute and they will pay your fare home, but your passport will be taken until the loan is repaid.

Changing money on the black market in places with weak or restricted currencies can be risky – don't do it unless you know what the risks are, and are prepared to take them.

Immunisation

Once you start travelling outside Europe, North America, and the rest of the so-called developed countries, you have to be

215

inoculated against the exotic diseases that lie in wait for unsus-
pecting travellers. It's best to start having the jabs at least 11
weeks before travelling, but if you are fit (and willing to feel
unwell for a while) they can be left up to 15 days before
departure. Your doctor should be able to do most of them (and
you will have to pay) or your travel agent will be able to advise
you on alternatives. At the end of it you should be presented
with the official International Certificate of Vaccination, which
you should keep with your passport to present when you enter
countries that require it and when you return to the UK.

Currently only cholera and yellow fever inoculations are
compulsory, and then only for certain countries, but the Department of Health leaflets 'Protect Your Health Abroad' and 'Health
Protection' will give you official requirements for all countries
and a list of immunisation centres in this country. (Ask for them
at the post office or your Community Health Centre.) Also, if
you book through a travel agent he will tell you what the
inoculation requirements are for your trip.

Working abroad

One way to pay for your visit to a foreign country is by working
there, but unless you've got skills that are very much in demand,
you'll find getting work abroad pretty hard, and the jobs you'll
get will tend to be the jobs the natives don't like, such as
temporary agricultural work (grape-picking etc), domestic or
au-pair work. For better paid jobs, especially for a longer stay,
get hold of the local papers (either subscribe or make a trip to
the relevant embassy), or consult a specialist employment
agency. If you have pen-friends, they can be asked to keep an
eye out for jobs. Students are eligible for various job exchange
schemes; your student union should have details.

Generally, most countries (except those in the EC) have legal
restrictions on foreigners working and you will need to get a
special visa from their embassy in Britain first. Together with the
usual problems of finding accommodation, the language bar-

rier, if it isn't an English-speaking country, and culture shock, this makes it an uphill struggle. If you're still interested, Vacation Work, 9 Park End Street, Oxford, publishes guides to working abroad. The Central Bureau for Educational Visits and Exchanges also publishes a guide, *Working Holidays Abroad*, available from their office at Seymour Mews House, Seymour Mews, London W1 (071-486 5101).

> **66**
>
> **Most countries have legal restrictions on foreigners working and you will need to get a special visa from their embassy.**
>
> **99**

Travel agents and tour operators

Travel agents can provide information and tickets for most trips and holidays. Do shop around between them as agents vary in their ability to get you discounts, flights when you want them, and guarantees against the collapse of tour companies (If you have booked a holiday with a tour company that goes bust, you can probably say goodbye to your money unless you have such a guarantee).

Most people take package holidays, which means you make one payment that covers the cost of travel there and back, the hotel and meals. Package holidays are convenient, simple and often cheaper than doing it yourself. But tour operators do vary a lot, and paying more isn't always a guarantee that you'll get more. Ask friends for recommendations, and do a bit of research (see next page). Brochures should be read with scepticism; they are rarely factually wrong, but frequently their descriptions don't say anything about the character of the places in them, or what sort of person they would suit. Read between the lines; for example, if you're going to a beach resort, and the brochure is not specific about how far the hotel is from the beach, then find out from the agent, because the brochures often only give the distance when the hotel is very close to the beach. Check also on whether the company will put up the price of the holiday if exchange rates or fuel costs change both at the time of booking and going – if not, the company will advertise a 'no surcharge guarantee', which means what you pay is *all* you pay.

Unfortunately, for unusual holidays such as specific interests or exotic locations, travel agents (except the more specialised ones) don't do so well, mainly because they often don't bother to refer to the comprehensive information back-up that is available to the travel trade. If the agent isn't obliging, you can find out about such holidays yourself in the reference section of larger libraries. A twice-yearly *Holiday Guide* (St James Press) lists all package holidays, tours, cruises, and special interest holidays. European hotels are listed in the *Agents' Hotel Gazetteer*, which rates both hotels and resorts. All scheduled flights (ones on fixed routes and times) are listed in the *ABC World Airways Guide*, a two-volume work which gives both schedules and fares. The *Faresavers' Guide* and the *Charter Guide* are aimed at agents who provide charter tickets. For shipping, ABC also do the *Shipping Guide*, but it doesn't cover all the Greek inter-island ferries, and for a quick guide to cross-channel ferries, see *Holiday Which?* (Consumers' Association). Thomas Cook publish a guide to Continental trains. General information is provided by ABC in their *Guide to International Travel*, and there is even a *World Weather Guide* (Hutchinson). *Holiday Which?*, published quarterly, can be relied upon for information about all aspects of travel – most libraries should have copies.

Cheap air travel

Once upon a time there were legitimate, official travel agents who sold expensive air tickets, and back-street 'bucket shops' which sold often exactly the same tickets at a huge discount. The travel agents hated the bucket shops, saying that they often defrauded their customers (which did happen, but not that often); the airlines abused them too, but still sold them discounted tickets in order to fill seats that might otherwise be empty. Nowadays the travel agents are allowed by their trade association, ABTA, to sell discount tickets to a limited extent, so the division is no longer so clear cut. The rule is, as always, to get quotes from several places, both official travel agents and the bucket shops. The latter advertise (occasionally with misleading prices) in local papers, some national papers and listings magazines.

Special conditions usually apply to cheap tickets. If you are getting an official concession ticket, it will probably be either an APEX or PEX or Excursion. With APEX, there is a limited number of seats available, advance booking (up to a month) is required, and you must stay a minimum of one week, and a maximum of three months. The minimum stay for PEX and Excursion is less, and the maximum stay usually three months. With other cheap flights you may find you are travelling at night and that there is no flexibility over the date of your return.

For most concession or cheap tickets you must pay in advance, and if you change your mind, or miss the plane (for whatever reason) you may lose your money, though you can take out insurance over this. You may be liable to surcharges, and might have to pay airport taxes; check these out.

If you do decide to go to a bucket shop, don't hand over anything apart from a small deposit until you see the ticket issued by the airline, and have checked that the dates, times and destinations are what you ordered.

If you can travel at short notice, and want to go to a holiday resort, keep an eye out in the travel agents' window or papers and listings magazines. Tour operators only make money by flying completely booked planes, so they will cut prices near the departure date if a plane isn't full.

It is inadvisable to buy a ticket off someone who is unable to use it, as tickets are not transferable. On most international flights airlines check the name on the ticket against that on the passport.

Hotels and guest houses

In Britain comprehensive lists of hotels, guest houses and bed and breakfast places are kept at local tourist information offices, and you can turn up in a town and just go to the office. If you want to get names and addresses before you go, your local tourist information office, or the British Tourist Authority (071-730 3400) should be able to give you the local contact point. Booking in advance is advisable in summer, but at other times of the year it is not really necessary unless you want a particular hotel that may be popular.

If you're going overseas, and you're not using a travel agent to book you a hotel, most national tourist organisations (both in their London and local offices) have comprehensive lists of hotels, often with grades and comments. Most hotels on the Continent are price-controlled, with the room price being featured on official lists, in the hotel foyer, and in the room itself. It is accepted practice in Europe that you can have a look at a room before you take it – certainly worth doing in cheaper places. Unlike Britain, the price quoted is not usually per person but per room, though often with a supplement for extra people, so two can often stay almost as cheaply as one.

As in Britain, you can get details of local hotels from a tourist office. To find it look for a blue sign with the letter 'i', or ask the police. There are many unofficial hotels and guest house guides – one of the best is the American 'Let's Go' series, which is specifically aimed at younger people.

Youth Hostels

Youth Hostels, at least in the UK, are the cheapest alternative to camping or sleeping rough. The average price for a 16–20 year old staying one night in a standard hostel is £4.00.

Internationally, there are 5,000 hostels in over 50 countries, but in other countries hotels may be just as cheap, especially if you're travelling with another person. However, even then hostels have certain advantages – you can be reasonably certain the accommodation is clean and adequate, and there are often cooking facilities, which can be a blessing in countries where it is expensive to eat out. (Most hostels can provide cooked meals and packed lunches if required.) You can meet other travellers, as most hostels have common rooms where you can sit and chat, and they will often be your best source of information. Moreover, hotels and guest houses can be a bit alienating after a while. Against that, hostels can occasionally be far from city centres, and inaccessible by public transport; they have rules about the earliest you can check in (usually early evening) and the latest (almost always before midnight); and you almost always have to sleep in dormitories, which can be hell if you're a light sleeper in with a clutch of snorers. Hostels are almost always shut during the day, which can be annoying if you want to rest or avoid the rain.

You need to have your own pillow-case and two sheets or a sheet sleeping-bag, but these can be hired. Many hostels (especially on the Continent) only open in the summer season, so do check the opening hours and dates.

It costs £4.00 to join the Youth Hostel Association for England and Wales, £2 for the Scottish YHA if under 18 and £5 if over, and £3 for the YHA of Northern Ireland if you're under 18, £7 if over. The YHA also has a travel agency, YHA Travel, with branches in London, Manchester, Birmingham, Cardiff, Cambridge, Staines and Oxford.

Hitching

Hitching is a way of travelling free, except that, as they say, nothing in life is ever really free. In this case, most drivers pick you up because they are bored, and your payment is in conversation.

Dress smart and smile if you want to travel fast. Pick a spot that allows drivers to see you (and examine you) in time, and stop for you in safety. Carry as little luggage as possible, and show a destination sign if possible. Getting out of large towns can be a problem, so most hitchers get public transport to the city limits. It's illegal to hitch on the motorways (or their Continental equivalents), though it's generally OK on slip roads or service areas.

> **Most drivers pick you up because they are bored, and your payment is in conversation.**

Hitching can be dangerous, especially if you are a female, so be careful when you accept rides. If in doubt when someone stops for you, ask where they are going first and then say you want to go in a different direction.

A good map is essential, especially on the Continent. *Europe – a Manual for Hitchhikers* by Simon Calder (Vacation Work) gives country-by-country advice and has motorway maps which show good hitching points.

Travelling almost free

If you do not want to pay commerical rates for your journey, but don't fancy hitching, you can try 'drive aways' – cars that the owners/operators/agents want taken somewhere else. However, you generally have to be over 21, and pay for the petrol (and have a clean driving licence, of course). There may be other costs too. Ring the large car rental chains for details.

For really long distance travel, especially across the Atlantic, air courier companies (listed in the Yellow Pages under 'Courier Services') often need people to accompany packages on the plane. The deal varies from company to company, and often all you get is some reduction in the air fare.

Cars, motorbikes, mopeds

Cars can be expensive to run, so it's worth sitting down with pen and paper if your budget is going to be tight to see whether you can afford it, and if so, how much you can pay. You have to allow not just for the purchase price of the car and petrol, but tax (currently £100 a year), insurance (more if you are young), repairs and servicing. Each year the AA produces figures for the average running costs of a car, including depreciation – the amount it loses in value each year. The figures vary according to the size of the car, but start at around 30p per mile. So a car that does 10,000 miles a year is costing its owner around £3,000 per annum. Bikes and mopeds cost less, but the danger of accidents, especially on motorbikes, is far greater. For the age at which you are allowed to drive see p.130.

Which car or bike

The Consumers' Association does regular tests on cars that are published in *Which?*. Your local library should have copies. This is probably the best way to find out about a model's reliability, running cost, comfort and performance. Motorbikes are reviewed in *Which Bike?* and *Bike Magazine*; for mopeds consult *Which?* also.

Learning to drive

Driving lessons are expensive – £8 an hour is fairly normal. You could get a patient relative or friend to teach you, but even then you need at least a few lessons just before the test, as instructors know what examiners are looking out for. If you are being taught by a relative or friend, before you get annoyed with them for shouting at you for nearly going through a red light, bear in mind that they may have had to increase their insurance payments to cover a learner driver.

The Star Rider scheme is universally recommended for prospective motorcyclists, and effective instruction is very important here as the accident rate is so high. Your local motorbike shop will have details of where to enrol.

Buying second-hand

If you don't have a knowledgeable friend to help you buy a car or bike, join the AA or RAC, as they provide a cheap vetting service which will give you a thorough report on a car. *Which?* is a good source of information about which car makes and models have long-term reliability problems.

When buying second-hand off a dealer, get in writing what sort of guarantee they offer, and if you have problems with the dealer over any faults you find later (even if you don't have a guarantee) see your local Citizens Advice Bureau (CAB). *Exchange and Mart* (or for motorcyclists, *Bike Buyers Guide* or *Motorcycle News*) will give you a good guide to prices. If you buy a vehicle off a private individual, your rights are far more limited if anything goes wrong than if you buy from a dealer, but if that private individual makes a hobby (or business) out of buying and selling cars, the law may treat him as a dealer.

When buying privately, it's always worth checking carefully that what you're being sold actually belongs to the seller. Ask to see the original receipt. You can find out whether the car really belongs to a finance company by getting your local CAB to check on your behalf. Generally, if you buy something that the seller doesn't own, you may lose it and not get any money back. However, if you buy a car that turns out to belong to a finance company despite the seller assuring you (preferably in writing) that it doesn't, you may be able to keep it – once again, consult your CAB.

Finance

If you can't put up cash, a dealer can usually arrange finance, irrespective of whether the car is second-hand or new. Before you accept, check whether you could get a cheaper loan from a bank (see p.105).

Insurance

It is compulsory to have at least third party insurance for any car or motorbike you own – this means that you are protected from claims by other road users. The point of this is to protect other people, because if you knock somebody down on a crossing and seriously injure them, they may successfully sue you for a large sum in compensation, but you are very unlikely ever to have such a large sum of money to pay them. With third party insurance the insurance company will pay up for you.

Most people take out either third party, fire and theft, or comprehensive insurance, all of which cost more, but cover you for more than the basic insurance. The former means that you are also covered to the value of any damage done to the vehicle by a fire or its loss if stolen, while the latter means that you are covered for any damage to you or your vehicle, even if you are to blame. Insurance is very complex and every company has different definitions of what is a bad risk, so it is worth getting quotations from at least three companies. Premiums cost more if you're under 25, if you've got a more powerful vehicle, or one that is more expensive to repair. They even vary according to your job and where you live.

Legal requirements

Apart from third party insurance, all cars and motorbikes must be registered and licensed (taxed). Registration should be done by the dealer if new; if second-hand the seller should give you the registration document (commonly called the 'log book') which will give details on how to transfer the record of ownership to your name.

Licensing forms are obtainable from post offices. When applying you have to show the insurance certificate or temporary cover note, and the MOT certificate if the car is over three years old, as well as filling in the form. MOT (for 'Ministry of Transport') certificates certify that a car is fit to go on the road, and are issued by qualified garages. The certificate costs £10.70;

you also have to pay if the car fails. Licensing costs £100 per year for a car, and from £10 to £40 for mopeds and motorcycles, depending on size.

Accident liability

If you're involved in an accident, try and remember the following:

1 Keep calm, even if the other party is at fault.
2 Don't admit blame – it may invalidate any insurance policy you have.
3 Get witnesses – take names and addresses.
4 Get driver's name, address, and the car's registration number, plus, if possible, the name of his or her insurance company. If a parked car contributed to the accident, take its number as well.
5 Draw a sketch map of the area showing what led up to the accident.
6 List the damage to yourself, your vehicle and anything else.
7 Inform the police, especially if anyone has been hurt or public property (for example, a bollard) damaged, as this is a legal requirement.

If the other party was clearly at fault, and there are witnesses to this, his or her insurance company should pay for any damage to you or your car. If the fault was yours, or if you cannot prove it was the other person's, your insurance company will only cover your losses if your insurance is comprehensive. Even then it is not worth claiming if the cost of repair is very small as you will lose your no-claims bonus – the discount given on your insurance premium for not having made a claim.

Maintenance

Try local night classes if you want to learn how to do it yourself; also most libraries have various repair manuals you can borrow. If you take the vehicle to a garage, always give precise instructions; for servicing, say you want the 'x mile service' as specified by the maker; for repairs, specify the symptoms you want fixed, and say that you must be notified before they start work on something you haven't told them about. It avoids arguments if you get an estimate of the cost before the job is started, preferably in writing. Check the final bill carefully – if the garage does work you didn't authorise, you don't have to pay for it. If you have a complaint and the garage is unhelpful, contact your local CAB.

Selling

Exchange and Mart is a good guide to what you should ask if selling privately; if selling to a dealer, get quotes from a few others. If you sell privately, don't let the prospective purchaser drive the car on his or her own, and not even with you in the car without checking that they are covered by insurance. Especially don't take anything but cash or a banker's draft if the buyer wants to take the vehicle right away. If you take a cheque, insist on a small cash deposit as well (just in case the cheque bounces, and you have to re-advertise the vehicle), and wait until the cheque is cleared by the bank before parting with the vehicle.

[U]SING YOUR TIME

You probably think you don't need any advice on how to use your time, but once you've left school 'free time' takes on a new meaning, depending on whether you're starting work, continuing your education or you're still looking for a job. If you're starting a job you may be surprised by how little time you've suddenly got for outside pursuits, and how tired you are when you get home. Most jobs involve an eight or nine hour day even if it's not set out in the traditional 9 to 5 time scale, and you may have to do a certain amount of overtime. If you're doing shift work or 'unsocial hours' (which can mean almost anything other than the usual 9 to 5) how you use your time will depend on your actual hours – you may find that this sort of working is in fact more flexible.

Going on to college or training may give you more time to yourself, although some vocational and training courses keep you pretty busy all day (see p.66). However you'll find that higher education establishments expect you to organize your own time (see p.75). College life does have its own momentum, though, and there's usually plenty of distraction from study.

If you're unemployed and not on a training scheme then you'll have a lot of time on your hands. The 'Unemployment' chapter outlines lots of schemes for using your time constructively so that it actually raises your chances of getting a job but some of the suggestions given here might interest you too.

Adding skills

No matter what your circumstances, you can always learn to do something different – or perfect something you're already interested in. Adult education institutes and the Workers' Educational Association (see p.74) are both good sources of part-time courses run both in the day and in the evening for anything from carpentry or agricultural engineering to life-drawing, drama or beginner's Russian. Some will be free if you're unemployed, others might charge a nominal fee. They are never expensive, and some are run especially for women.

Courses are changing all the time, new schemes and projects specific to your area are starting up. Keep in touch, and save yourself some of the effort and legwork and money by using the services there to help you. Your local education authority should have an advisory service which will be in touch with all the opportunities in your area; use their free advice and information service.

Using the library

One of the best sources of information for all local initiatives, work-shops, training programmes and educational opportunities is the library. The main library in your area will probably have a worker dealing specifically with young people and if not will at least be able to guide you where to look for more information. And the library is a fantastic source of information and interest in other areas. (You'll find many references to 'your local library' as a source of reference for information of all sorts elsewhere in this book.)

You are entitled to join the nearest public library to your place of residence. All you need to take with you is proof of identity (a rent-book, driver's licence, benefits book, etc) and you can join on the spot and take out books and other materials.

Unpaid work

There are basically two types of unpaid work. Organised voluntary work, whether long or short term, which is usually to do with helping others, and work that you hustle for yourself to gain experience in your chosen field. Even if you've already got a job, it may not be exactly what you want, so doing a bit extra for free in a different environment can help you change direction.

It's up to you to organise this type of work yourself. Offer your services to the local hospital/theatre/arts centre/shop/political organisation/paper/OAP home/playgroup/charity or recording studio, factory or workshop. If you're short of ideas of who to approach, talk to your local youth club worker or youth officer (see p.233). Ask around – your parents or your other older friends or relations may well have ideas. It gives you valuable work experience and also adds to your personal 'achievement chart'.

Voluntary work

Voluntary work may conjure up a picture of worthy ladies organising jumble sales – and while there's nothing wrong with that, it's an image that's out of date. Whether you're working, studying or unemployed, giving your time for the benefit of other people can be rewarding, useful, helps you gain skills and experience in a variety of fields, gets you out of the house, and so is never a waste of time.

Before you decide who to volunteer with, ask yourself how much time can you give to it. Just a few evenings now and then? Full-time for a summer or more? The answers will help you channel your energies into a suitable outlet.

For what's available on a regular short-term basis in your area, contact the local Volunteer Bureau, or Community Service Volunteers (look in the phone book for your local office, or contact their head office at 237 Pentonville Road, London N1 9NJ; 071-278 6601). Or contact the Young Volunteer Resources Unit, 17–23 Albion Street, Leicester LE1 6GD, or get the 'Youth Action Volunteer List' from the Young Volunteer Bureau (as above). Some of the voluntary work projects listed in the chapter on 'Unemployment' may also be suitable for students or those in work, if the voluntary work involves evenings, weekends or shortish periods which could be taken as holiday.

Political parties and pressure groups are always crying out for volunteers to raise money, canvass opinion, address envelopes or whatever. See p.121 for more details.

In the longer term summer workcamps are organised by the International Voluntary Service, 1 Belvoir Street, Leicester LE1 6SL (0533 541862) and usually involve a summer's work (six weeks to three months) at a camp either in Britain or elsewhere in Europe. They organise work like conservation and archaeological projects, playschemes, providing and supervising holidays for the mentally or physically handicapped. Food and accommodation are provided, and the schemes are a good way of developing skills, an opportunity to meet lots of people from other countries and a chance to get to Europe. And they look good on a job application form.

Community Service Volunteers is the largest long-term voluntary work organiser in the UK. Anyone from age 16–35 can apply for a place on a project that might involve work in a home or a hospital, a shelter for the homeless or on a community project. No one is rejected and the schemes can last for four to twelve months. Write to the Community Service Volunteers, 237 Pentonville Road, London N1 9NJ (071-278 6601) for details. But if you're unemployed, don't forget that long term projects such as these may affect your elegibility for benefits (see p.57).

Earning extra cash

If you've got a job, the chances are you'll be at the bottom of the wage scale. Your income from social security at 16–18 is even less, and if you're a student your grant won't go far once you've paid for board and lodging, books and travel. But there are ways of using your time to add to this amount. Of course, if you've been doing a Saturday or evening job for some time, you'll already have some ideas about earning extra cash. But maybe you could be doing something else. Think of what you enjoy doing yourself, and how to expand it. Could you do photography for other people, paint, decorate, make clothes, or jewellery, or food, and sell it? Sell yourself and your services as a childminder/window cleaner/gardener? What about getting together with a group of friends, pooling your resources and trying to make some money in that way. Look through the local Yellow Pages or classified ads section of the paper. What services aren't being offered? Could you provide them?

> **66**
>
> **Could you do photography for other people, paint, decorate, make clothes, or jewellery, or food, and sell it?**
>
> **99**

Ask your local youth worker for any more suggestions. Contact the National Youth Bureau (address on p.240) for more ideas on what other young people in other areas have got involved with. Take this idea a step further and you are considering becoming self-employed – making it on your own. You might want to consider this as the work you do builds up and you think you can survive on it alone, or if you've got some cash behind you already, but what you'll need in both cases is advice and guidance. See the 'Self-employment' chapter. Ask at the careers office for help, or at the local Chamber of Commerce. There's a free Small Firms Information Service you can reach via the telephone operator, and the library and local Training Agency (which also runs a number of 'enterprise schemes' – see phone book) will have books on starting and running a business.

Time for pleasure

'Leisure' is a word which means different things to different people, and you'll probably already have favourite leisure activities. But if you want to widen your scope a bit, the ideas mentioned below are just a few examples of what might be available in your area, and what to do if they're not. Use the library to find out what else is on offer.

Every local authority has an area Youth Officer who you can contact through the council offices or the local education authority. The youth officer keeps a register of all youth groups, youth clubs and centres, and projects aimed at young people. They might put out a regular newsletter listing activities and events.

" . . . so with all this spare time I thought I'd build a friendly bank manager."

Neighbourhood projects and day centres may not appear to be particularly youth orientated, but again, will be involved in interesting issues and projects related to your area, as well as providing good social meeting places.

Find out from the library if there are any women's groups or gay or lesbian groups in your area if this is what interests you.

Don't forget sport

Now that you're no longer being told when and what to play doesn't mean you should dismiss sport out of hand; it isn't just good for you, it's fun. You could just go and watch of course, but it's often cheaper to join in. Think of all the sports you've fancied trying but didn't get the chance to – archery, fencing, diving, karate, mountaineering, bowling, snooker – and you'll probably find there are clubs and groups running them in your area. They might be free, or charge just a minimal fee to cover costs. Ask at the library. Apart from informal contacts for football and cricket teams, the best places to find out about sport are the council offices and your nearest sports centre. The local council may run coaching courses and events in a variety of sports; ring the recreation officer at the main council office.

Find out where the local sports centre is, if you don't already know, see what sports they offer, and if they don't do the one you want, suggest it. If you're going to use the centre frequently, it's worth joining to cut down on costs and enjoy preferential bookings. If you're unwaged, ask about concessions and free coaching. If they don't offer concessions, get on to the local council, ask them why not, and get your friends to do likewise. If you're at college you'll probably find you've got access to good facilities (see p.77). Private clubs are growing, but are a lot more expensive, and don't usually offer concessions to unwaged people. But their facilities are usually good; many have restaurants and bars and so double as social meeting places. If you get a job in a large company you may well find they have recreational facilities, possibly even their own sports centre on site. Ask the personnel officer when you start work.

If you still can't find the sport you want, ring the Sports Council (071-388 1277). They'll have a list of national and local contacts. Or think about starting your own group with friends, and encourage the local sports centre to let you use their facilities on favourable terms.

Getting away

There are a number of independent schemes and organisations for young people run and funded either through charities, trust funds, industry or central government. The library should keep details of them all and the conditions of participation; this is just a selection of the more well known.

- The Outward Bound organisation runs courses in canoeing, climbing, walking and so on, in Wales, the Lake District and Scotland. There is a charge, but they do have a bursary fund to help applicants who can't afford the costs.

- The Duke of Edinburgh's Award: a programme of leisure time activities that aim to challenge young people between the ages of 14–25.
- The STA Schooners Scheme: founded by Sir Winston Churchill, it takes 39 young people on a round-the-world sailing trip every year.
- The British Association for the Advancement of Science has 100 branches round the country, and runs groups for young people with an interest in science.

If you are interested in the Armed Services, you'll find most run youth sections, or volunteer sections. Their numbers should be in the telephone directory, or ask at the library.

Good times

Find out what's coming up at the nearest art gallery, theatre, cinema or concert hall from the library or the local paper. There are so many free newspapers now that you probably won't have to pay for a newspaper that gives you this sort of information.

Your area should have a tourist information office; they're often one of the best sources of local 'What's On' information, especially in the country, and they're not just for outsiders. Churches often put on non-religious performances of various kinds (even pop concerts) especially in rural areas, so look at the parish noticeboard. Cinemas and theatres usually have a cheap night, or standby tickets, or offer concessions to students and those on benefits (see p.61). Youth clubs, drop-in centres, women's and gay and lesbian groups often organise free showings of films, so keep in touch. If you live in a rural area with poor transport, see if there's a film society or similar run locally in the school, village hall or even the pub (you'll probably have to be 18 to join the latter, but not necessarily). If not, why not try to organise one yourself with a group of friends? Your local librarian could give you details on how to go about this (or any such similar activity) and it beats staying at home watching videos night after night.

If you can sing or play a musical instrument there are lots of amateur choirs, bands and orchestras who are glad to recruit newcomers. The local church is an obvious starting-point especially for a choir, but the library will probably have details of other local groups. If you're new to an area and want to play or hear rock music or jazz, pubs are often the best venues for cheap – or even free – gigs. Look in newspapers and listings magazines for details.

It beats staying at home watching videos night after night.

You are probably already familiar with the local pub, club and winebar scene – and their exorbitant prices. But if you are finding out about them for the first time, don't forget the licensing laws, which forbid anyone under 18 to drink wine, beer or spirits without a meal. And look out for dress codes; some clubs are very particular about the 'type' of client they want in them. Try and avoid hassles with bouncers by checking this, and also entrance fees, before you go. It's worth shopping around for cheap nights as well, or cheap entrances before a certain time – and ask if they offer any concessions.

Gambling and amusement arcades

Gambling is tempting if you've got a bit of cash, but it really is a mug's game. You have to be 18 to gamble whether it's with a race-course bookie, in a betting shop, a bingo hall or a classy casino. Bookies and betting shops are freely accessible but bingo halls and casinos usually charge an admission fee – quite high in the case of casinos. These latter will also probably have minimum stakes, which may be £5 or higher.

As gambling is strictly governed by law, you're likely to be shown the door pretty sharpish if the manager thinks you're under age, as he or she won't want to lose his or her licence. No matter what anyone says, in the end gambling is a sure way to lose money. It can be as additive as alcohol or smoking, and even more expensive, so if you think your gambling is becoming a problem, or you know someone else with this problem, get in touch with Gambling Anonymous.

More and more amusement arcades are springing up and filling their premises with young people out of work and with nothing to do during the day. Like betting shops, they must be one of the quickest places to watch your cash disappear. It's really easy to get into the habit of having 'one last go' to try to recuperate your losses. They can be good meeting places, but try and avoid the trap of spending all your money and time in them; look back at this section for alternative ways to fill your time.

Religious groups

If you belong to one of the mainstream religions you probably already have a church, synagogue or temple which you attend regularly. When you move away from home you will normally find that there is a place of worship of your denomination or sect within reach (look in the phone book if you do not find one by walking around). They usually have youth sections. Colleges and universities generally have at least Christian and Jewish fellowships. If you want to find out about a particular religion or just want to worship from time to time, you can usually just turn up for a service.

Most religions are keen to accommodate volunteers, so if you wish to do more than just worship you will find that there is plenty to do to spread or administer your faith. This sort of work also provides the opportunity to develop your social contacts with like-minded people.

Alternative religions

Many people now look for spiritual development outside the traditional religious organisations. A great variety of paths are offered, calling for different degrees of commitment of your time.

For instance, the original purpose of yoga was as a spiritual discipline, and many organisations teach it with the aim of leading to meditation. Meditation is also taught, in a form that doesn't involve yoga, by various organisations such as the International Meditation Society ('Transcendental Meditation'), the School of Meditation and smaller groups revolving round one particular teacher.

You may find that you have been stopped in the street at some time by an evangelical member of one of the more 'extreme' sects, and if not you will almost certainly have heard something about 'the Moonies' (the Unification Church), the Children of God, the Scientologists, the Hare Krishna Movement and other such cults. These call for total commitment from their followers, including in some cases going to live with them, handing over part of your income and changing your name. If you are considering joining one, think very carefully first about how much it will change your life, and look hard at your reasons, particularly if you are acting emotionally because you happen to be down or depressed at the time you are approached.

Most of these organisations advertise their meetings in the local newspapers, in listings magazines, and in local libraries. They can also be found in the phone book under the name of the organisation.

USEFUL ADDRESSES

NB Where possible, important addresses have been given in the text. The following list is by no means comprehensive, but will supplement those addresses already given and will help you to extend your contacts in a number of fields.

Employment, education and training

Agricultural Training Board, Summit House, Glebe Way, West Wickham, Kent (081-777 9003)

Careers and Occupational Information Centre (COIC), Moorfoot, Sheffield S1 4PQ

Careers Research and Advisory Centre (CRAC), Bateman Street, Cambridge (0223 354551)

Central Council for National Academic Awards (CNAA), 344-5 Gray's Inn Road, London WC1X 8BP

Commission for Racial Equality (CRE), Elliott House, Allington Street, London SW1E 5EH (071-828 7022)

Disablement Information and Advice Line, The Flat, Park Grange, 100 Park Grange Road, Sheffield S2 3RA (0742 727996)

The Equal Opportunities Commission (EOC), Overseas House, Quay Street, Manchester 3 (061-833 9244)

EOC Northern Ireland, Lindsay House, Callender Street, Belfast BT1 5DT (0232 42752)

The Law Centres Federation, Duchess House, Warren Street, London W1 (071-387 8570)

The Low Pay Unit, 9 Upper Berkeley Street, London W1JH 8BY (071-262 7278/9)

The National Advisory Centre on Careers for Women, Artillery House, Artillery Row, London SW1 (071-799 2129)

The National Extension College, 18 Brooklands Avenue,
  Cambridge CB2 2HN (0223 316644)
National Council for Civil Liberties (NCCL), 21 Tabard
  Street, London SE1 (071-403 3888)
The Trades Union Congress (TUC), 26 Great Russell Street,
  London WC1 (071-636 4030)
The Training Agency, Moorfoot, Sheffield S1 4PQ
  (0742 753275)
Welsh Development Agency, Youth Training Centre,
  Treforest Industrial Estate, Pontypridd, Mid-Glamorgan
  (0443 841191)

Business enterprise and self-employment

Association of British Chambers of Commerce,
  212 Shaftesbury Avenue, London WC2H 8EB (071-240 5831)
Centre for Employment Initiatives, 140a Gloucester Mansions,
  Cambridge Circus, London WC2 (071-240 8901)
The Co-operative Development Agency, Broadmead House,
  21 Panton Street, London SW1Y 4DR (071-839 2985)
The Council for Small Industries in Rural Areas (CoSIRA),
  141 Castle Street, Salisbury, Wiltshire SP1 3TP (0722 336255)
The Highlands and Islands Development Board, Bridge House,
  20 Bridge Street, Inverness IV1 1QR (0463 234171)
The Industrial Common Ownership Movement, Vassalli House,
  20 Central Road, Leeds LS1 6DE (0532 461737)
Livewire, Freepost, Cambridge CB2 1BR (0223 316156)
Local Enterprise Development Unit, Upper Galwally, Belfast 8
  (0232 690131)
Mid-Wales Development, Ladywell House, Newtown, Powys,
  SY16 1JB (0686 626965)
Small Firms Service, Dial 100 and ask for Freefone 2444
National Federation of Self-Employed and Small Businesses,
  333 Garstang Road, Fulwood, Preston, Lancs (0772 716038)
Scottish Business in the Community, Queen Margaret
  College, Clerwood Terrace, Edinburgh EH12 8TY
  (031-317 7366)

The Scottish Co-operative Development Committee,
  Templeton Business Centre, Templeton Street, Bridgeton,
  Glasgow G40 1DA (041-554 3797)
The Welsh Development Agency, Small Firms Centre,
  Wood Street, Cardiff (0222 396116)
Young Enterprise, Ewert Place, Summertown, Oxford OX2 7BZ
  (0865 311180)

Unemployment, voluntary work and leisure

British Association for the Advancement of Science,
  Fortress House, 23 Savile Row, London W1 (071-494 3326)
British Unemployment Resource Network, 318 Summer Lane,
  Newtown, Birmingham B19 3RL (021-359 3562)
Central Bureau for Educational Visits and Exchanges,
  Seymour Mews House, Seymour Mews, London W1
  (071-486 5101)
Church Action with the Unemployed, Hollywell Centre,
  1 Phipp Street, London EC2 (071-729 1434)
Community Service Volunteers, 237 Pentonville Road,
  London N1 9NJ (071-278 6601)
Duke of Edinburgh's Awards, 5 Prince of Wales Terrace,
  London W8 5PG (071-937 5205)
International Voluntary Service, 1 Belvoir Street, Leicester
  LE1 6SL (0533 541862)
National Council for Voluntary Organisations, 26 Bedford
  Square, London WC1B 3HU (071-636 4066)
National Youth Bureau, 17-23 Albion Street, Leicester LE1 6GD
  (0533 554775)
Outward Bound Trust, Chestnut Field, Regent Place, Rugby,
  Warwickshire (0788 60423)
Royal Jubilee Trusts for Community Activity, 8 Bedford Row,
  London WC1 (071-430 0524)
STA Schooners' Scheme, 2a The Hard, Portsmouth, Hampshire
  (0705 832055)
The Scottish Sports Council, Caledonia House, South Gyle,
  Edinburgh 12 (031-317 7200)

The Sports Council, 16 Upper Woburn Place, London WC1
(071-388 1277)

The Sports Council for Northern Ireland, House of Sport,
Upper Malone Road, Belfast BT9 6RZ (0232 381222)

The Sports Council for Wales, Sophia Gardens, Cardiff CF1 9SW
(0222 397571)

Voluntary Service Overseas (VSO), 9 Belgrave Square, London
SW1 8PW (071-235 5191)

Young Volunteer Centre, 23 St Albans Road East, Hatfield,
Herts (0707 261977)

Young Volunteer Resources Unit, 17-23 Albion Street,
Leicester LE1 6GD (0533 558763)

Money matters

Association of British Insurers, Aldermary House,
10-15 Queen Street, London EC4N 1TT (071-248 4477)

Banking Information Service, 10 Lombard Street, London
EC3V 9AR (071-626 8486/9386)

British Insurance Brokers Association (BIBA), 10 Bevis
Marks, London EC3 (071-623 9043)

The Building Societies Association (BSA), 3 Savile Row,
London W1X 1AF (071-437 0655)

The Consumers' Association, 2 Marylebone Road, London NW1
(071-486 5544)

The Insurance Ombudsman Bureau, 31 Southampton Row,
London WC1B 5HJ (071-242 8613)

The National Consumer Council, 20 Grosvenor Gardens,
London SW1 (071-730 3469)

Office of Fair Trading, Field House, 15-25 Bream's
Buildings, London EC4A 1PR (071-242 2858)

Personal Insurance Arbitration Service (PIAS), c/o
Chartered Institute of Arbitrators, International
Arbitration Centre, 75 Cannon Street, London EC4N 5BH
(071-236 8761)

Health and relationships

ACTS (Adolescent Confidential Telephone Service) (Dublin) 0001-740723/744133/729574. A help-line for young people to discuss problems about contraception, conception, relationships, pregnancy, etc.

The Accept Clinic, 200 Seagrave Road, London SW6 (071-385 2481). Advice, information and counselling for people with drinking problems.

Alcohol Concern, 305 Gray's Inn Road, London WC1 (071-833 3471). For access to a national network of local advice centres.

Alcoholics Anonymous, PO Box 514, 112 Redcliffe Gardens, London SW10 9BQ (071-352 3001); 152 Lisburn Road, Belfast (0232 681084); Wales: 0222 (Cardiff) 373939 (7pm - 10pm)

Alcoholics Anonymous Family Groups, 61 Great Dover Street, London SE1 4YF (071-403 0888)

Anorexia and Bulimia Nervosa Association, Annexe C, Tottenham Town Hall, London N15 (081-885 3936)

Anorexic Aid, The Priory Centre, Priory Road, High Wycombe, Bucks (0494 21431)

ASH (Action on Smoking and Health), 5-11 Mortimer Street, London W1N 7RI I (071-637 9843); 6 Castle Street, Edinburgh EH2 3AT (031-225 4725); 40 Eglantine Avenue, Belfast BT9 6DX (0232 663281)

ASHA (Asian Women's Resource Centre), 46 Myrdle Street, London E1 (071-375 2404). For help, support and comfort for Asian girls and women.

British Association for Counselling, 37a Sheep Street, Rugby, Warwickshire (0788 78328/9)

British Pregnancy Advisory Service (BPAS), 7 Belgrave Road, London SW1 (071-222 0985)

Brook Advisory Centre, 153a East Street, London SE17 2SD (071-708 1234 or 071-708 1390). Local branches are listed under "Brook Advisory Centre" in telephone directories.

Children's Legal Centre, 20 Compton Terrace, London N1 2UN (071-359 6251)

Equal Opportunities Commission, Overseas House, Quay Street, Manchester M3 3HN (061-833 9244)

Family Planning Association (FPA), 27-35 Mortimer Street, London W1N 7RJ (071-636 7866). Local clinics can be found in most areas and are listed under "Family Planning" in telephone directories.

Family Planning Association Northern Ireland, 113 University Street, Belfast BT7 1HP (0232 325488)

Gamblers Anonymous/Young Gamblers, 17-23 Blantyre Street, London SW10 (071-352 3060)

Gay Switchboard, 071-837 7324. A 24-hour support and advice line for homosexuals.

Gingerbread, 35 Wellington Street, London WC2E 7BN (071-240 0953). Self-help groups for single parents.

The Irish Family Planning Association, 59 Synge Street, Dublin 8 (0001 682420)

Incest Crisis Line, 66 Marriott Close, Bedfond, Feltham, Middlesex (071-890 4732)

Incest Survivors' Campaign, c/o The Woman's Place, Hungerford House, Victoria Embankment, London WC2 (071-836 6081)

National Association of Citizens' Advice Bureaux, Myddleton House, 115-123 Pentonville Road, London N1 9LZ (071-833 2181)

National Association of Young People's Counselling and Advisory Services (NAYPCAS), 17-23 Albion Street, Leicester LE1 6GD (0533 558763)

National Childbirth Trust (NCT), 9 Queensborough Terrace, London W2 3TB (071-221 3833). Write to them or phone them for details of your local branch.

National Council for One Parent Families, 255 Kentish Town Road, London NW5 2LX (071-267 1361)

Northern Ireland Association of Citizens Advice Bureaux, New Forge Lane, Belfast BT9 5NW (0232 681117)

Pregnancy Advisory Services (PAS), 11-13 Charlotte
Street, London W1 (071-637 8962)

Rape Crisis, PO Box 69, London WC1 XNJ (071-837 1600)

Release, 169 Commercial Street, London E1 (071-603 8654).
For help with drug-related problems.

Royal Association for Disability and Rehabilitation
(RADAR), 25 Mortimer Street, London W1N 8AB (071-637
5400)

Samaritans, listed in telephone directories under
'Samaritans'. They provide immediate emotional support
when you ring them.

Scottish Association of Citizens Advice Bureaux, 26
George Square, Edinburgh EH8 9LD (031-667 0156/8)

Scottish Community Education Council (SCEC), Atholl
House, 2 Canning Street, Edinburgh 3 (031-229 2433)

Scottish Health Education Group, Woodburn House,
Canaan Lane, Edinburgh ED10 4SQ (031-447 8044)

Ulster Pregnancy Advisory Services, 719a Lisburn Road,
Belfast 9 (0232 381345)

Women's Health Information Centre, 52 Featherstone
Street, London EC1 (071-251 6580)

Housing and accommodation

Advisory Service for Squatters, 2 St Paul's Road, London N1
(071-359 8814)

Alone in London Service, 188 King's Cross Road, London WC1
(071-278 4224)

CHAR (Campaign for the Single Homeless), 5-15 Cromer Street,
London WC1 (071-833 2071). Local groups are listed
under "CHAR" in telephone directories.

Housing Advice Switchboard, 47 Charing Cross Road, London
WC2 (071-434 2522)

National Federation of Housing Associations, 175 Gray's
Inn Road, London WC1 (071-278 6571)

National Tenants Organisation, c/o National Consumer
Council, 20 Grosvenor Gardens, London SW1 (071-730 3469)

Piccadilly Advice Centre, 100 Shaftesbury Avenue, London W1 (071-437 1579)

SHAC (The London Housing Aid Centre), 189a Old Brompton Road, London SW5 (071-373 7841)

SHELTER, 88 Old Street, London EC1 (071-253 0202); 57 Walter Road, Swansea (0792 469400); 103 Morrison Street, Edinburgh (031-229 8771); 23a University Road, Belfast (0232 247752)

YMCA (headquarters), 16 Great Russell Street, London WC1 (071-580 4827)

YMCA National Council, 640 Forest Road, London E17 (081-520 5599)

Political organisations

Parliamentary parties

The Conservative Party, Central Office, 32 Smith Square, London SW1P 3HH (071-222 9000)

The Labour Party, 150 Walworth Road, London SE17 1JT (071-703 0833)

The Liberal Democrat Party, 4 Cowley Street, London SW1 3NB (071-222 7999)

The Green Party, 10 Station Parade, Balham High Road, London SW12 (081-673 0045)

The Social Democratic Party (SDP), 28 Buckingham Gate, London SW1 (071-630 1772)

Plaid Cymru, 51 Cathedral Street (Heol yr Eglwys), Cardiff CF1 9HD (0222 231944)

The Scottish National Party (SNP), 6 North Charlotte Street, Edinburgh EH2 4JH (031-226 3661)

The Democratic Unionist Party, 296 Albert Bridge Road, Belfast 5 (0232 458597)

The Ulster Unionist Party, 3 Glengall Street, Belfast 7 (0232 224601)

The Social Democratic and Labour Party (SDLP), 38 University Street, Belfast 7 (0232 223428)

Sinn Fein, 51-3 Falls Road, Belfast 12 (0232 323214)

The European Community

The European Parliament Information Office, 2 Queen
Anne's Gate, London SW1H 9AA (071-222 0411)

The European Commission, 8 Storey's Gate, London SW1
(071-222 8122)

UK Permanent Representative to the EEC, 6 Rond Point
Schuman, 1040 Brussels, Belgium (010 322 230 6205)

Some well-known pressure groups:

Amnesty International, 5 Roberts Place, London EC1
(071-251 8371)

British Union for the Abolition of Vivisection (BUAV),
16a Crane Grove, London N7 (081-700 4888)

Campaign against Arms Trade, 11 Goodwin Street, London N4
(071-281 0297)

Campaign for Freedom of Information, 3 Endsleigh Street,
London WC1 (071-278 9686)

Campaign for Nuclear Disarmanent (CND), 22-4 Underwood
Street, London N1 (071-250 4010)

Child Poverty Action Group, 1 Bath Street, London EC1
(071-253 3406)

The Disability Alliance, 25 Denmark Street, London WC2
8NJ (071-240 0806)

Friends of the Earth, 26 Underwood Street, London N1
(071-253 0201)

Greenpeace, 30 Islington Green, London N1 (071-354 5100)

Youthaid, 17 Brownhill Road, London SE6 (081-697 2152)

F URTHER READING

NB Important books and pamphlets are mentioned in the text where relevant. Those listed below may help with extra information, but we don't pretend it is a comprehensive list. (The addresses of many of the organizations who have produced these books are listed under 'Useful Addresses'.)

British Government and Politics R. M. Pannett (Heinemann Educational Books)

The Careers Book Klaus Boehm and Jenny Lees-Spalding (Macmillan)

Choosing at 16 (Dept. of Education and Science free leaflet)

Commons Select Committees Edited by Dermot Englefield (Longman)

The Context of British Politics David Coates (Hutchinson)

Decisions at 15-16 Michael Smith (CRAC)

Directory for the Disabled (RADAR)

The Directory of First Degree Courses (CNAA)

Directory of Jobs and Careers Abroad (Vacation Work)

Disability Rights Handbook

Family Money Nigel Smith (Adamson Books)

Finding a Place to Live in London (Housing Advice Switchboard)

Focus at 18 (Newpoint)

Gays at Work (Gay Rights at Work Committee)

Gay Workers, Trade Unions and the Law (NCCL)

A Great British Institution: The Commons Today Edited by S. A. Walkland and Michael Ryle (Fontana)

The Guardian Guide to Running a Small Business Clive Woodcock (Kogan Page)

A Guide to Housing Benefit (SHAC)

The Guide to Non Means-tested Social Security Benefits (CPAG)

Immigration and Race Maggie Wilson (Pelican)

The International Directory of Voluntary Work (Vacation Work)

Introduction to British Politics John Dearlove and Peter Saunders (Polity Press)

Kibbutz Volunteer (Vacation Work)

Local Government: Politicians, Professionals and the Public in Local Authorities Howard Elcock (University Paperbacks)

Making It Happy Jane Cousins (Penguin)

Mastering British Politics F. N. Forman (Macmillan)

Moneyfacts (COIC)

National Welfare Rights Handbook (CPAG)

Nice Work if You Can Get It Guy Dauncey (National Extension College)

People and Politics in Britain Lynton Robins, Tom Brennan and John Sutton (Macmillan)

Politics of Pressure: The Art of Lobbying Malcolm Davies (BBC Publications)

Office Workers' Survival Handbook Marianne Craig (BSSRS)

Rights at Work Jeremy McMullen (Pluto Press)

Safety and Health at Work (TUC)

Second Chances for Adults (National Extension College)

The Small Business Kit (National Extension College)

So You Want to Stop Smoking (ASH free leaflet)

Streetwise Judith Lowe, Isabel Wright and Michael Finn (BBC Publications)

Talking Sex Dr Miriam Stoppard (Piccolo)

The UCCA Handbook (UCCA)

The Unemployment Handbook Guy Dauncey (National Extension College)

Volunteer Work Abroad (Central Bureau for Educational Visits and Exchanges)

Well-being: Helping Yourself to Good Health Robert Eagle (Penguin)

Women's Employment Rights (Labour Research Department)

Women's Rights in the Workplace Tess Gill and Larry Whitty (Pelican)

Women's Work, Women's Health (WEA)

Work for Yourself (National Extension College)

Work Your Way Around the World (Vacation Work)

Your Choice at 17+ Michael Smith and Peter March (CRAC)

Your Choice at A-levels (CRAC)

INDEX